HISPANIC TEXTS

*general editor*
Professor Catherine Davies
Department of Spanish, Portuguese and Latin American Studies
University of Nottingham

*series previously edited by*
Professor Peter Beardsell, University of Hull
Emeritus Professor Herbert Ramsden

*series advisers*
*Spanish literature*: Professor Jeremy Lawrance
Department of Spanish, Portuguese and Latin American Studies,
University of Nottingham
*US adviser*: Professor Geoffrey Ribbans, Brown University, USA

*Hispanic Texts* provide important and attractive material in editions with an introduction, notes and vocabulary, and are suitable both for advanced study in schools, colleges and higher education and for use by the general reader. Continuing the tradition established by the previous *Spanish Texts*, the series combines a high standard of scholarship with practical linguistic assistance for English speakers. It aims to respond to recent changes in the kind of text selected for study, or chosen as background reading to support the acquisition of foreign languages, and places an emphasis on modern texts which not only deserve attention in their own right but contribute to a fuller understanding of the societies in which they were written. While many of these works are regarded as modern classics, others are included for their suitability as useful and enjoyable reading material, and may contain colloquial and journalistic as well as literary Spanish. The series will also give fuller representation to the increasing literary, political and economic importance of Latin America.

# Mientras los hombres mueren

Manchester University Press

HISPANIC TEXTS

Carmen Conde

*Mientras los hombres mueren*

edited with an introduction, critical analysis, notes and vocabulary by
**Jean Andrews**

Manchester University Press
Manchester and New York
*distributed exclusively in the USA by Palgrave Macmillan*

The right of Jean Andrews to be identified as the author of this work has been asserted
by her in accordance with the Copyright, Designs and Patents Act 1988.

*Published by* Manchester University Press
Oxford Road, Manchester M13 9NR, UK
*and* Room 400, 175 Fifth Avenue, New York, NY 10010, USA
http://www.manchesteruniversitypress.co.uk

*Distributed exclusively in the USA by*
Palgrave, 175 Fifth Avenue, New York, NY 10010, USA

*Distributed exclusively in Canada by*
UBC Press, University of British Columbia, 2029 West Mall,
Vancouver, BC, Canada V6T 1Z2

*British Library Cataloguing-in-Publication Data*
A catalogue record for this book is available from the British Library

*Library of Congress Cataloging-in-Publication Data applied for*


ISBN 978 0 7190 7752 4 *paperback*

First published 2009

18  17  16  15  14  13  12  11  10  09      10  9  8  7  6  5  4  3  2  1

The publisher has no responsibility for the persistence or accuracy of URLs for
external or any third-party internet websites referred to in this book, and does not
guarantee that any content on such websites is, or will remain, accurate or appropriate.




Typeset in Adobe Garamond Pro
by Koinonia, Manchester
Printed in Great Britain
by Bell & Bain Ltd, Glasgow

# Contents

Carmen Conde by the Guadalquivir, near
Jaén, 13 June 1937. Courtesy of the Patronato
Carmen Conde-Antonio Oliver.

I fought in hills near Teruel.
I was so cold and hungry. Who was foe or brother
No-one learnt. Black mounds under the snow
Were bodies or else earth.[1]

[1] Sheila Wingfield, *Beat Drum, Beat Heart* (1946) in *Collected Poems* (London: Enitharmion, 1983).

# Preface

## Carmen Conde and *Mientras los hombres mueren*

Carmen Conde was a poet, novelist, children's writer, dramatist, biographer and historian. She was a champion, with her husband, of the legacy of the Nicaraguan *modernista* Rubén Darío, a great friend and source of encouragement to generations of women poets younger than herself, and the first woman elected to the Spanish Royal Academy in modern times. She was a complex, sometimes difficult woman who lived a life which was wholehearted in its commitment to the people she loved and the causes she believed in. She remained steadfast in her efforts to maintain allegiances, both personal and political, across divides considered unbridgeable by those who demand of human life that it be separable into black and white, right and wrong, with us or against us.

The affectionate and fulsome description of Conde five years before her death, at the age of 89, provided by Encarna León in her introduction to Conde's recollections of her childhood in Melilla, *Empezando la vida*, offers some insight into this woman of many facets:

> Mucho y muchos han hablado sobre su carácter, su forma de ser. Aunando criterios podría decirse que ella es: firmeza y ternura, sinceridad, calidad poética, mediterránea, tremendamente española, de temperamento fuerte y melancólico, mística, de voz penetrante, luminosa, ardiente, cósmica. Luchadora, altiva, espontánea, de gran valor moral, rebelde ante la injusticia, generosa ...[1]

*Mientras los hombres mueren* is a collection of prose poems rooted in her experience of conditions during the Spanish Civil War which Conde wrote in Valencia between 1937 and 1939. They describe, in haunting terms, the responses of a woman contemplating the deaths of the men at the front and observing the annihilation of children in cities bombarded by sea and air. She was in her early thirties at the time. The poems were not published in their entirety in Spain until 1967 when they were included in a collected edition of Conde's poetry, *Obra poética*, edited by Emilio Miró.[2] She republished the sequence in her three-volume autobiography,

[1] Encarna Leon, 'Presentación', Carmen Conde, *Empezando la vida: Memorias de una infancia en Melilla (1914-1920)* (Melilla: UNED, 1991), pp. 11-14, p. 13.

[2] Emilio Miró (ed.), *Obra poética de Carmen Conde* (Madrid: Biblioteca Nueva, 1967; 2nd ed. 1979), pp. 185–215.

*Por el camino, viendo sus orillas*, in 1986, incorporating it into the narrative as a chapter bearing witness to her experiences during the Civil War.[3]

There are many reasons which might explain why this poetry has not reached prominence. If it had been published and circulated in the Republican zone during the Civil War then the poetry might have become part of the established Republican Civil War canon, as was the case, most notably, with the work of her close friend, Miguel Hernández. It must be said, however, that during the Civil War poets on both sides of the ideological divide, whose work had been deliberately elitist and abstract in the 1920s and early 1930s, made a determined effort to produce poetry which would be accessible both rhythmically and intellectually to the masses.[4] Conde, on the other hand, appears to have been spurred in the opposite direction. Her first two collections, though both in the minor form of prose poetry, *Brocal* (1929) and *Júbilos* (1934), were lyrical, amenable and, at least on the surface, simple, much in the manner of Juan Ramón Jiménez' much-lauded and widely-translated *Platero y yo* (1914). However, in *Mientras los hombres mueren*, she developed a dense, complex, often angular prose, which is, in most of the poems, packed solid with several layers of imagery. There is no indication, with the exception of one poem, *La guerra en el puerto*, that she was, in any sense, writing these poems to fulfil any function other than a deeply personal one at the time.[5] When the poetry was eventually published in Spain, prose poetry had long fallen out of fashion. Thirty years after the Civil War, in 1967, it was still also possibly too soon for an overlooked work of such lacerating intensity to be drawn to the public's attention. The same might be said of its second appearance in 1986.

Perhaps now, twenty years further on, in a climate of restitution and openness in Spain regarding the events of the Civil War, *Mientras los hombres mueren* will finally find its place. It has already made a very welcome reappearance in Emilio Miró's definitive edition of Conde's collected poetry which was published in 2007, the year of her centenary.[6] This collection remains the most significant single work of poetry by a woman to emerge from the Civil War itself and the most substantial apolitical collection by any Spanish poet of note from the war period.[7]

[3] Carmen Conde, *Por el camino, viendo sus orillas*, 3 vols (Barcelona: Plaza y Janés, 1986), I, pp. 165-191.

[4] See César de Vicente Hernando, 'Estudio Preliminar', *Poesía de la guerra civil española 1936-39* (Madrid: Ediciones Akal, 1994), pp. 5–36. This anthology contains poetry published during the Civil War in Spain and abroad.

[5] No. XXXIV of *Mientras los hombres mueren*, 'La guerra en el puerto', was read out to the dockers of El Grau on 15 December 1938.

[6] Emilio Miró (ed.), *Carmen Conde: Poesía completa* (Madrid: Editorial Castalia, 2007), pp. 159–178.

[7] Much of the poetry written by poets living in war zones, on both sides, was published exclusively in newspapers and magazines. Very little was produced in book form. Rafael Alberti's, *Capital de la gloria* and the far lesser-known Lucía Sánchez Saornil's *Romancero de mujeres libres* offer two instances where occasional war poems were collected in a volume and published during the war years. *Capital de la gloria* was written under siege conditions in Madrid between 1936 and 1937 and published in *De un*

# Acknowledgements

I should like, first and foremost, to thank the Ayuntamiento de Cartagena, Patronato Carmen Conde-Antonio Oliver and its director, Cayetano Tornel Cobacho, for permission to reproduce in this edition the text of *Mientras los hombres mueren* and other materials provided to me in manuscript form by the Patronato. I am also grateful for permission to reproduce the photograph of Carmen Conde (in Jaén in 1937). I should like especially to express my gratitude to Caridad Fernández Hernández of the Patronato for her warm welcome when I visited the Patronato and for her unfailingly generous help, expertise and advice throughout the preparation of this edition.

I am indebted to the Department of Spanish, Portuguese and Latin American Studies at the University of Nottingham for funding my visit to the Patronato and for allowing me study leave to work on this edition. I am particularly beholden to my colleague Catherine Davies, a much-respected pioneer in the field of women's writing in Spanish, for her support and encouragement in this venture.

Finally, I should like to thank the staff of Manchester University Press for their forbearance and professionalism.

---

*momento a otro* (Madrid: Ediciones Europa America, 1937; it appears with additional poems written in 1938 in *Poesías completas*. Buenos Aires: Losada, 1961, pp. 410-423). Much of this poetry is occasional in the truest sense, celebrating the achievements and sacrifices of individuals or groups and other significant events. Lucía Sánchez Saornil, an *ultraísta* poet in her youth and a prominent figure in the anarchist movement in the 1930s published her *Romancero de mujeres libres* in 1937 (Valencia: Ediciones Mujeres Libres, 1937). As the title suggests, it is a brief collection of ballads devoted to the public evocation of prominent figures and battles. Miguel Hernández, the poet of the Spanish Civil War par excellence, was widely published in newspapers and magazines between 1936 and 1939. However, the only collection to appear during the war itself was *Viento del pueblo, Poesía en la guerra* (Valencia: Socorro Rojo Internacional, 1937). The remainder of his war poetry was collected in *El hombre acecha* (in press by 1938 but never actually published) and *Cancionero y romancero de ausencias* (poetry written between 1939 and 1941 and not published in any form in his lifetime). The poetry of *Viento del pueblo* and *El hombre acecha* is public poetry, engaged with the lives and the suffering of soldiers and the political events of the times. The poems of *Cancionero y romancero de ausencias* are much more inward and reflective. (See *Miguel Hernández, Poemas sociales, de guerra y de muerte*, ed. & prologue, Leopoldo de Luis (Madrid: Alianza, 1989).)

xi

# Introduction

## The Spanish Civil War (17 July 1936–1 April 1939)

In an article published in the *Observer* on 22 March 1959, close to the twentieth anniversary of the end of the Spanish Civil War, Sebastian Haffner, the German historian and journalist, one-time editor-in-chief of the *Observer* newspaper and himself voluntarily exiled from Nazi Germany in 1938, sums up a perception of the events of the war then current in Western European democracies. To the non-specialist, these views are relevant, and indeed dominant, even now:

> To middle-aged liberals, the Spanish civil war, which ended twenty years ago, brings back memories of the strongest political emotions they probably felt in their lives. Battle-names like Badajoz, Guadalajara, or Teruel, still tear at their heartstrings after all this time. To them, 'Spain' was a fight of good against evil.
>
> A hopeful, young democratic republic brutally attacked by black military reaction, heroically defended for almost three years by its almost bare-handed people, and in the end trampled underfoot with the help of Moors and Foreign Legionaries, German Nazis and Italian Fascists, while the democracies supinely looked the other way and played 'the farce of non-intervention': this was the picture then, this is still the memory now.[1]

Haffner goes on to elaborate on the complex nature of the conflict in Spain, an assessment which now, forty years after his article appeared, is taken as read by all serious historians and commentators in Spain and elsewhere, both in print and online.

Indeed, the word memory now, in the first decade of the twenty-first century, carries the universal connotation of memory studies and the recovery of the unrecorded past. In the case of Spain, the past decade has seen a process of opening-up with regard to discussion of and research into the experience of the Civil War defeated under the dictatorship. It has involved the testimony of the defeated and their families and a panorama

[1] Sebastian Haffner, 'Spain – The Legend and the Reality', *Observer*, 22 March 1959.

of research projects on and celebrations of the portions of the story so far untold. The judicial and political culmination of this movement took place in November 2007, when, under the Socialist government of José Luis Rodríguez Zapatero, the *Ley orgánica de la memoria histórica* was approved by the Spanish Congress (*Congreso de Diputados*) and passed to the Senate for formal ratification. In a parallel act of restitution, which may not altogether be the rather astonishing coincidence it might appear to constitute, on 28 October 2007, the Vatican beatified 498 martyrs of the Civil War, almost all of these clergy killed in the Summer of 1936 under the 'Red Terror'.

The *Ley orgánica de la memoria histórica* is designed to right the wrongs perpetrated throughout the Franco Regime and to recognise, at last and before it is too late, the contribution and suffering of the defeated. The rationale of the Zapatero government is as follows:

> Es la hora, así, de que la democracia española y las generaciones vivas que hoy disfrutan de ella honren y recuperen para siempre a todos los que directamente padecieron las injusticias y agravios producidos, por unos u otros motivos políticos o ideológicos o de creencias religiosas, en aquellos dolorosos períodos de nuestra historia. Desde luego, a quienes perdieron la vida. Con ellos, a sus familias. También a quienes perdieron su libertad, al padecer prisión, deportación, trabajos forzosos o internamientos en campos de concentración dentro o fuera de nuestras fronteras. También, en fin, a quienes perdieron la patria al ser empujados a un largo, desgarrador y, en tantos casos, irreversible exilio. Y, por último, a quienes en distintos momentos lucharon por la defensa de los valores democráticos, como los integrantes del Cuerpo de Carabineros, los brigadistas, los combatientes guerrilleros, cuya rehabilitación fue unánimemente solicitada por el Pleno del Congreso de los Diputados de 16 de mayo de 2001, o los miembros de la Unión Militar Democrática, que se autodisolvió con la celebración de las primeras elecciones democráticas.[2]

That thirty years should have elapsed since the Transition to Democracy in Spain (1976–1978) before such a law, which also finally and formally legitimises the actions of all those engaged in covert and proscribed opposition to the Franco regime during the dictatorship, could be promulgated is a reflection of the nature of the accommodation arrived

---

[2] Carlos E. Cué, 'La ley de memoria se aprueba entre aplausos de invitados antifran-quistas', *El País*, 10 November 2007. The full text of the law, 'Proyecto de Ley por la que se reconocen y amplían derechos y se establecen medidas en favor de quienes padecieron persecución o violencia durante la Guerra Civil y la Dictadura. (10.10.07)' is also included in the print and online edition of *El País* for this date.

at during the Transition: the cultivation in political and cultural circles of an attitude of 'desmemoria', a reluctance to delve too deeply into the injustices of the past for fear of destabilising a democratic future which, arguably, was only secured after the abortive military coup attempt of 23 February 1981 (*23–F*) and the left-wing PSOE (Partido Socialista Obrero Español) general election victory on 28 October 1982. Unsurprisingly, this pragmatic, many would say cynical, approach was much criticised within and outside Spain. Indeed, in a piece published as late as 1995, the legal scholar Elías Díaz lamented this culture of 'collective amnesia *vis-à-vis* the past' suggesting that at best it may be seen as 'the well-intentioned if mistaken idea that "consensus" depends on the obliteration from memory of past divisions' and at worst it constitutes 'a politically interested denial of the past'.[3] The long dictatorship and the tacit pact of 'forgetting' which, to some extent, underpinned the Transition are not, however, perhaps the only reasons for the long political silence.

Quite apart from the considerations of public discourse and political life, the toll on human beings of involvement as soldiers or citizens in war is only just beginning to be understood in all its ramifications. There was no trauma counselling for combatants and civilian victims of war in the 1930s and 1940s, no name for what is now recognised as Post-Traumatic Stress Disorder. The generation that fought and suffered in Spain and those who endured the horrors of the Second World War, each in their individual humanity marked by the unspeakable, found their only refuge to be silence and self-containment. It is only now, as these men and women, the survivors, are in their eighties and nineties, that the floodgates are being opened and what has remained locked away for seventy years has somehow, finally, been rendered utterable.

Since the millennium, there has been a spate of novels in Spain, written by the grandchildren of those who lived through the Civil War as young adults, which attempt to understand, recover or give voice to the ordeals of that scarred generation. Arguably, the most notable of these, is Javier Cercas' *Soldados de Salamina* (2001), a novel which has been widely translated, including into English, and made into an internationally distributed film by David Trueba in 2003.[4] The conditions which have

---

[3] Elías Díaz, 'The Left and the Legacy of Francoism: Political Culture in Opposition and Transition' in Helen Graham and Jo Labanyi (eds), *Spanish Cultural Studies: An Introduction* (Oxford: Oxford University Press, 1995), pp. 283–294, p. 288.

[4] Javier Cercas, *Soldados de Salamina* (Barcelona: Tusquets, 2001); David Trueba, *Soldados de Salamina* (Warner, 2003).

evolved to make this novel a runaway popular and critical success are patently circumstances which ought to produce a sympathetic audience for Carmen Conde's long-overlooked *Mientras los hombres mueren*.

The total death toll during the Spanish Civil War is generally taken to be of the order of half a million, though all sources admit it may never be possible to arrive at an accurate figure. This figure includes combatants, civilians, and those either executed or assassinated. During the war, those civilian deaths which were not due to bombardment, starvation or illness were occasioned by the 'Red' and 'White' terrors. Some 38,000 people were killed in the Republican zone, mainly in the first few months after the outbreak of the war, largely because, as Antony Beevor observes, there was an 'almost total lack of control in the first days of the rising', this in spite of the persistent 'attempts by left-wing and Republican leaders to stop the violence'.[5] Those deemed disloyal to the Republican government, those whose actions or conduct before the war had caused injury, hardship or worse, or those unlucky enough simply to fall foul of one faction or another allied to the Republican cause were either executed or assassinated by extreme elements within the Republican family (a spectrum running from liberal republicanism to anarchism via moderate socialism, bolshevism, Trotskyism, communism, anarchism and anarcho-syndicalism and also including Basque and Catalan nationalism). Many clergy were also killed in an opportunistic heightening of the anti-clericalism and church-burning which had been part and parcel of the birth of the Republic, and indeed which had broken out sporadically in parts of Spain over the previous century.

It is worth noting, in this context, that by the early 1930s, Spain had one of the lowest church attendance ratings of all the Catholic nations of Europe.[6] This reality, paradoxically, took nothing from the political and symbolic power of the Church and the highly emotive nature of response to it on both sides of the political divide, both at the level of popular reaction and political debate.[7] The first Republican government introduced reforms effectively disestablishing Catholicism as the state religion: abolishing the subsidies previously paid by the state to the Church, laicising education and introducing civil marriage, civil burial

[5] Antony Beevor, *The Battle for Spain: The Spanish Civil War 1936–1939* (London: Penguin, 2006), p. 86.

[6] See Frances Lannon, *Privilege, Persecution and Prophecy: The Catholic Church in Spain* (Oxford: Clarendon Press, 1987), pp. 9–36.

[7] Beevor, *The Battle for Spain*, p. 25.

and divorce. However, this does not, at the same time, imply that all those who were Republicans were also by default atheist or anti-clerical, far from it. For example, the first president of the Republic, Niceto Alcalá Zamora, of the centre right Derecha Liberal Republicana, was a practising Catholic as of course were the vast majority of Basque nationalists allied to the Republican cause. Nonetheless, it was inevitable that the temporal Church would identify itself, from the outset, with the anti-Republican insurrectionists (*sublevados*) and that its authority figures and a majority of clergy on the ground would contribute in a significant way, though there were many notable exceptions, especially in the Basque country, to the representation of the uprising as a holy crusade undertaken to return Spain to the Mother Church. Thus, at the end of the war, Eugenio Pacelli, the now discredited Pope Pius XII, was able to 'give sincere thanks with your Excellency [Franco] for the victory of Catholic Spain'.[8]

It was usually with the full blessing of local and national clergy that the Nationalist 'white terror' effected a wave of purges which, in its ruthless disregard for human life, would rival any excess of Stalinism. Summary executions and imprisonments were more often than not publicly sanctioned by the local Catholic priest who would be a member of the committee set up to sentence all those suspected of Republican sympathies once an area had fallen to the Nationalists. The purging was methodical and sustained, 'partly to destroy the democratic aspirations encouraged under the Republic and partly because they had to crush a hostile majority in many areas of the country'.[9] Once they had taken possession of an area, the Nationalist army would execute union leaders, mayors, civil governors and other government representatives. Even military officers of the highest rank who had remained loyal to the legitimate government were declared traitors, denied the usual right of a court martial and declared guilty and shot as 'rebels'. Those captured at the front, regular soldiers, militia and civilians were also, customarily, shot there and then. When the army had moved on, the Falange would move in (in some areas this task would be carried out by Carlists) and carry out a purge of lower level members of the community: members of parliament and government officials, left-wing party officials, even ordinary members and those who worked for those parties in relatively apolitical functions such as typists. Doctors, lawyers, teachers, intellectuals, Freemasons, perceived and actual, were

---

[8] Beevor, *The Battle for Spain*, p. 397.
[9] Beevor, *The Battle for Spain*, pp. 88ff.

also targeted. 'In fact, anyone who was even suspected of having voted for the Popular Front [the left-wing government elected on 16 February 1936] was in danger'.[10] These killings continued for some time after the war ended. In total, it is now estimated that about 200,000 people were put to death by Nationalist forces during and after the war.

This does not take into account those who died in concentration camps and prisons in Franco's Spain through malnutrition, enforced dehydration, unsanitary conditions and crippling hard labour. While on 19 May 1939, '120,000 soldiers – including legionnaires, *regulares*, Falangists and *requetés* [Carlist militia] –' took part in the victory parade which strode down the grand boulevard of the Castellana in Madrid (renamed Avenida del Generalísimo), up to 500,000 of the defeated were incarcerated in prisons and temporary transit camps.[11] Many more would be denounced, executed or imprisoned, guilty or not, over the next ten years while those who had, in any sense, been sympathetic to the Republic would find themselves cast out of teaching and other government posts, and virtually unemployable in all but the most menial tasks. Most monstrously of all, however, the regime also took it upon itself to remove children from parents with histories of even mild left-wing activism in order to 're-educate' them in state and religious institutions, often 're-homing' them with families with unimpeachable Francoist credentials.[12]

Children also suffered greatly during the war itself. According to the Spanish Ministry of Labour and Social Affairs, the number of children killed in the Civil War is of the order of 138,000.[13] As this was the first war where aerial and naval bombardment of civilian populations was employed as a major tactic of war, the forerunner of *blitzkrieg*, it was equally the first conflict in which there was a concerted attempt to send children to safety, either within Spain itself, away from vulnerable urban centres, or abroad.[14] This measure was undertaken, exclusively, on the

[10] Beevor, *The Battle for Spain*, p. 89.

[11] Beevor, *The Battle for Spain*, p. 400, p. 404.

[12] Beevor, *The Battle for Spain*, p. 407.

[13] 'Los niños de la guerra', Ministerio de Trabajo y Asuntos Sociales, DGE-SGONI, 11/05/2006, accessed on www:ciudadaniaexterior.mtas.es. All the information on this matter is taken from this piece and from 'Los niños de la guerra', Asociación Guerra, Exilio y Memoria Histórica de Andalucía at www:andaluciaymemoria.org.

[14] Bombing raids on civilian populations had been developed as a tactic of war by the German Air Force in the First World War. They used Zeppelin airships between 1915 and 1916 and after that bomber aircraft. The first Zeppelin bomb fell on London on 15 May 1915. From 23 May 1917, the Germans dispatched Gotha bombers first in daylight and then at night in raids over London. In the1930s, the development of air

Republican side. At the end of 1937, there were 564 *colonias escolares*, children's educational camps, in rural parts of the Republican zone, mainly in Catalunya and the Levante, in which were housed up to 45,000 children. From September 1936, children were also sent abroad to sympathetic countries. In the first formal arrangement between governments, 450 Spanish children were sent to the island of Oléron, off the coast of western France, on 20 March 1937. After the bombings of Guernica and Bilbao in the summer of the same year, as the Basque country was on the point of falling to the Nationalists, massive expatriations of children were organised by the Basque authorities. The vast majority of Spanish children were sent to France, Great Britain, Belgium and the USSR, although some also went to Switzerland, Scandinavia and Mexico. Three times as many children were evacuated in early 1939 as the war was coming to a close. It is estimated that in total 30,000 were sent abroad during the war and 90,000 in the immediate aftermath. Many of these children either chose not to return to Spain after the war, were encouraged by their parents not to return to the land of the 'defeated' or were not allowed by their host nations to return. This was the case with respect to children sent to Mexico and the USSR. Of those who did return, not all were reunited with their parents. A significant number, whose parents were deemed themselves to be undesirable elements, were placed in harshly run orphanages, later, in many instances, to be adopted by families approved by the regime. The same fate awaited those whose parents were either dead or untraceable. Sibling groups were split without a thought to the trauma the children had already been through. Many were even deprived of their first names. Since under the Franco regime, a Catholic baptismal name was de rigeur, all those who had been given secular first names, such as Libertad or Solidaridad, by more idealistic Republican or socialist parents were baptised with new, acceptably Christian first names. The story of these lost 'niños de la guerra', these days in their seventies, many separated forever from their blood relatives, is only now being told. In January 2005, the Spanish government awarded a fourfold increase in state pension entitlement plus guaranteed free health care in Spain to those Spanish nationals and 'niños de la guerra' still resident in other countries.

It goes without saying that women faced a complete reversal of legal status under the Franco regime. The first Republican government

---

power strategy and bomber aircraft technology would become the defining military priority of the Fascist dictatorship in Germany.

introduced the most complete legislation in favour of women then opera-
tive in any European democracy: they were entitled to vote, at a voting age
of 23, the same as for men; they were allowed to own property in their own
right, married or single, and to will it to their descendants; they had the
right to divorce and to work outside the home after marriage. However,
as Helen Graham notes, Spain in the 1930s was still a primarily agrarian
and deeply traditional society, where, apart from a few urban and socially
elite enclaves, a woman's place was still very much in the home, within a
conservative and patriarchal social structure.[15] Even on the extremes of
left-wing politics, women still played second fiddle and were expected to
take care of all the domestic duties on top of their paid work or public
political commitments, while their 'compañeros' (either common-law or
civil-marriage husbands) unselfconsciously preached women's equality at
anarcho-syndicalist or communist gatherings.

During the war itself, on the Republican side there was a certain number
of women directly involved in battle at the front, the *milicianas*, while
many more worked in munitions factories and other aspects of war work
and took men's places in a range of essential farming and urban-mainte-
nance tasks. On the Nationalist side, women were not openly involved in
war work, unless it was in the traditional areas of looking after children
and other social care roles. Many took part in the running of the various
women's activities within Falangism; most of these were selected by virtue
of family or marital relationships with male figures within the organisation. The most notable example of this was Pilar Primo de Rivera, director
of the Sección Femenina of the Falange, whose father was the military
dictator Miguel Primo de Rivera who had been ousted in 1930 while her
brother, José Antonio Primo de Rivera, was the founder of the Falange.
After the war, the Sección Femenina would run much of the social care
system in Spain and almost every woman would fall under its influence,
through the obligatory requirement to do six months' *servicio social* (the
female equivalent of conscription).[16] Under the Franco dictatorship, Pilar
Primo de Rivera would be the most powerful woman in the country in
her own right, since her brother had been executed by government forces
in November 1936. However, despite her unquestioned position, at
least one section of Falangism could not resist the atavistic temptation

[15] See Helen Graham, 'Women and Social Change', *Spanish Cultural Studies*, pp. 99–
115.
[16] See Helen Graham, 'Gender and the State: Women in the 1940s', *Spanish Cultural
Studies*, pp. 182–195.

of reducing her to the status of a sexual/political pawn. As she was an ardent Germanophile and apologist for Spanish entry into the Second World War in support of the Axis powers, it was at one point mooted that a marriage should be brokered between Pilar Primo de Rivera and Adolf Hitler, as a means of establishing a Hispano-German fascist dynasty along the lines of the Habsburg alliances of Spain's Golden Age of Empire. The overture was made in October 1941 by the fascist ideologue and writer Ernesto Giménez Caballero to Magda Göbbels, wife of Dr Josef Göbbels, the Nazi propaganda minister, at a private meeting during a fascist writers' gathering. Primo de Rivera, though not averse to the idea, declined on the grounds that she did not wish to sacrifice her personal life completely and that she did not consider herself worthy of such an honour.[17] She was born in the same year as Carmen Conde and was 34 in October 1941. Hitler, his unformalised alliance with Eva Braun notwithstanding, was 52.

Before the war, there had been prominent female politicians on the left, most notably Frederica Montseny, the Anarchist leader and first woman to be appointed to a cabinet post in Spain (in November 1936), the socialist Margarita Nelken, the Republican Victoria Kent (Director-General of Prisons 1931–32) and, of course, the communist, Dolores Ibárruri, la Pasionaria. Women were also present:

> in political action across the ideological spectrum (electoral campaigning, meetings, demonstrations), in the labour sphere (union bureaucracies and state arbitration committees), in the press (both as subjects of features and as journalists), on the radio, in the university sector, and sometimes in the gaols as political prisoners.[18]

As the rights accorded to women under the republic were completely rescinded by the Franco regime, they found themselves once more legally dependent on male relatives and obliged to give up formally contracted work on marriage. Many working-class women and widows of all backgrounds had no choice but to resort to the informal sector. Of these, more than a few were forced into that most informal sector of all, prostitution. Even so, for women, as for men, there were two Spains. For those women of the appropriate political hue, there was fulfilment within the activities of the Sección Femenina and satisfaction in restored family life and religious certainty:

[17] Wayne H. Bowen, 'Pilar Primo de Rivera and the Axis Temptation', *The Historian* (I: 67 (Spring) 2005), pp. 62–72, p. 68.
[18] Helen Graham, 'Women and Social Change', p. 109.

As Republican women were being shaved and dosed with castor oil by the 'victors' of their villages or transported across Spain with their children in cattle trucks in scenes of Dantesque horror, women in the Sevillian aristocracy or Salamanca bourgeoisie celebrated the 'redemption' of their private family sphere and revelled in the tremendous upsurge of public Catholic ceremonial.[19]

## Carmen Conde 1907–96

Carmen Conde Abellán was born in Cartagena on 15 August 1907 into a well-off and respectable middle-class family involved in the furniture and jewellery business.[20] She had an elder sister, Magdalena, born in 1897, who died at the age of nine months. After that, Conde's mother, María de la Paz Abellán García, suffered several miscarriages and was eventually strongly advised by her doctors not to attempt further pregnancies. However, she persisted and Carmen was born ten years after Magdalena. For the first seven years of her life, Carmen Conde had all the benefits that wealth, comfort, servants and doting parents could offer an only child. In 1914, however, the idyll came to an end. Her father, Luis Conde Parreño, a jeweller by trade, had, on his return from military service in the Philippines in 1898, begun to build up a business buying and selling furniture and jewellery which in no time brought him sufficient wealth to afford a large house, servants and a car. However, while he was lucky in his early efforts, he was not a natural businessman and eventually his lack of business sense allied to his generosity, indolence and taste for good living meant that in 1914 the business had to be declared bankrupt. The consequences for his family came swiftly. They lost house, car and servants almost overnight and he was obliged to move them to the Spanish enclave of Melilla, in Morocco, where he was given, as a last resort and through family connections, a position as jeweller/goldsmith in a department store. In better times, he had been reluctant to devote himself to jewellery-making because he feared the constant close work would cause him to lose his sight. At this stage, he had no choice. Even so, the family fortunes went

[19] Helen Graham, 'Gender and the State', p. 183.
[20] Most of the factual biographical information on Carmen Conde in this introduction is to be found in brief in Caridad Fernández Hernández, 'Cronología' in Francisco Javier Diez de Revenga (ed.), *Carmen Conde: Voluntad creadora* (Murcia: Sociedad Estatal de Conmemoraciones Culturales, 2007), pp. 57–66, and at much greater length in José Luis Ferris, *Carmen Conde: Vida y pasión de una escritora olvidada* (Madrid: Temas de hoy, 2007).

from bad to worse during the seven years they spent in Melilla. María de la Paz Abellán went from the initial indignity of selling her jewellery to the ultimate humiliation of doing her own laundry by hand, at a time when only peasant women and the urban poor did without the services of a washerwoman.

Conde herself seems to have thrived in North Africa and, in 1955, published a highly engaging memoir about her time as a young girl in Melilla, *Empezando la vida*, subsequently republished in 1991.[21] At that time, Melilla offered a society which, to the sensitive eyes and ears of the young Conde, hearkened back to what Spain might have been like before the Reconquest of 1492 and the Expulsion of the Jews. She had friends who were like herself, Spanish-born *peninsulares*, whose families were temporarily posted, for a variety of reasons, to Melilla, most rather better off than herself. She also had friends among the North African Jewish community and attempted to befriend, when she could, poor Arab children as well. She was very conscious of the divide between *peninsulares* and indigenous North Africans, and indeed of the relative nature of her own so-called poverty at the time. She tells a story of how a poor Arab child, attempting to beg in a *peninsular* neighbourhood, was roughly told to go away: 'Largo de aquí, vete, monta!'. As Conde comments, 'España era fuerte, mandaba'. She explains how the child, whom she names 'África', walks away, hungry and barefoot. She, however, would have liked to give the child all her own bread for nothing in return (if the adults would let her) because of her own thirst for knowledge about the continent on which she lives: 'Porque yo, "espaniola" pobre, quería andarla toda, y la niña de los palmitos se sabía todos los caminos'.[22]

At the same time, she recounts another tale which demonstrates her affinity with the poor among the Jewish community in Melilla. Carmen became attached to a Jewish woman called Luna who used to breast-feed her baby son in the street. Luna was renowned in the area for her beauty, but it seemed no-one among the *peninsulares* thought to concern themselves about her destitution. Conde goes home one day and tells her abstracted father that Luna's baby has died. His response disappoints her:

'... esa hebrea tan guapa que le daba de mamar en medio de la calle? ...' [...]

[21] Carmen Conde, *Empezando la vida: Memorias de una infancia en Marruecos (1914–1920)* (Tetuán: Ediciones Al-Motamid, 1955); Carmen Conde, *Empezando la vida: Memorias de una infancia en Melilla (1914–1920)* (Melilla: UNED, 1991), all quotes from this edition.
[22] *Empezando la vida* (1991), p. 60.

pero su mirada no comprendía nada: era la misma que cuando me mostraba los tesoros llegados de la Península: 'esas son tus joyas'. O cuando al ir por la calle se encontraba con una buena moza ...

No, a Luna no la sabía ver bien mi padre.[23]

Conde's father seems, at least in this telling, to have been a disappointment to her. The much-treasured family heirlooms which were eventually sent to Conde's parents in Melilla and destined to belong to Carmen meant absolutely nothing to the child herself, though they must have meant infinitely more to her bereft mother. She would have preferred her father to have been able to see beyond the surface of things, beyond class and race and the social mores which dictated bourgeois respectability even more acutely than the possession of jewellery. Her mother, however, whose own social background was inferior to her father's, appears, in contrast, to have had insight to spare. When the time came when she could no longer afford the services of Maimona, an Arab woman whom she had employed as laundress and general home help, María de la Paz Abellán's explanation of the matter to her daughter placed all the emphasis on Maimona's loss of income, not her own loss of comfort, referring to the innate dignity of a woman like Maimona and the iniquity of the life she was obliged to lead. Thus, Conde's recollection is of her mother's refusal to be anything other than compassionate to Maimona and her ilk even as the skin of her own once cosseted fingers was stung and split open by the harsh bleach she had to immerse her hands in to do the washing:

> Todos éramos pobres, sufrientes de perdidas comodidades peninsulares; pero Maimona, en su patria, era más pobre que ninguno. Vivía de servir-nos. Así lo aseguraba mi madre, tan fuerte y tan segura, que llevaba nuestra casa como un juguete (¡lejana madre sana y alegre en medio de los mayores esfuerzos y abnegaciones!)[24]

This tower of tolerance was, however, in other respects very much a creature of her times. She disapproved strongly of her daughter's interest in local Jewish and Arab children, and discouraged her attempts to learn Arabic or Hebrew, or to find out more about the ways of her little local friends. Undaunted as a child, when interviewed in her late seventies Conde remained caustic in her rejection of all the Christian Reconquest, and its much-heralded (especially by the Franco regime) female figure-head, Isabel la Católica, represented:

[23] *Empezando la vida* (1991), p. 65.
[24] *Empezando la vida* (1991), p. 67.

Me hice muy amiga de niñas hebréas [...] Y aprendí bastantes palabras del hebreo y del árabe. Sin embargo, para mi madre, castellana vieja, aquéllos eran los infieles [...] Mi madre, la pobre, que era tan buena y tan complaciente, se opuso terminantemente a que yo aprendiera el idioma de los infieles y me hablaba de doña Isabel [...] "Doña Isabel los echó", fue todo lo que me habían enseñado en el colegio de monjas. Nunca comprendí yo por qué doña Isabel *la Católica* fue tan obtusa que, cuando España se estaba desangrando con el descubrimiento de América, echó a los hombres que estaban arraigados y que producían riqueza auténticamente. Mi antipatía por esa señora no ha cesado todavía.[25]

Above all, in retrospect, Conde acknowledges that her life in North Africa, listening to the *cantoras*, the folk singers of the town, singing ballads which originated in the Spain of the Middle Ages and were brought to the North African coast by the Jewish diaspora, provided her with a living education in her own native culture as it was before the Expulsion, one which she was able to recognise and validate later on when she began her formal studies in literature:

¿Qué herencia depositó en mis venas el regusto por lo oriental? Muchos años después, al estudiar los romances, ¡cómo despertaron en su estancia olvidada las voces de aquellas cantoras del norte africano, primeras que me dieron lección de nuestro romancero, el que aún repiten con exactitud allá como en Salónica![26]

By 1920, the family's fortunes had recovered sufficiently for them to return to Cartagena. However, this was merely a partial amelioration and Conde was obliged to work for a living, once she reached the age of 16. She began work in the Drawing Office of the Sociedad Española de la Construcción Naval in Cartagena and passed the relevant state exams (*oposiciones*) to qualify and work as a draughtswoman. She remained in this post until the end of 1928.[27] At the time Cartagena was the headquarters of the Mediterranean Division of the Spanish Navy (Capital del Departamento Meditérraneo) and had been so since the early eighteenth century. It was therefore an important centre for shipbuilding and other maritime industry.

[25] Carmen Conde, *Por el camino viendo sus orillas*, 3 vols (Barcelona: Plaza y Janés, 1986), III, p. 260.
[26] *Empezando la vida* (1991), p. 54. Salónica is Salonika or modern-day Thessaloniki, the second-largest city in Greece. A large number of the Jews expelled from Spain and Portugal in the late fifteenth and early sixteenth centuries found refuge in Salonika, at the express invitation of the Ottoman rulers of the time.
[27] 'Prólogo' to *Ansia de la gracia* in *Obra poética* (1979), p. 244.

Conde began to publish prose in local newspapers and magazines, in Cartagena, Murcia and Lorca. In 1926, at the instigation of the editors of the local newspapers which published her work and under the guidance of Enrique Martínez Muñoz, the founder of the Escuelas Graduadas in Cartagena, the Ayuntamiento (Town Council) in Cartagena offered her a scholarship covering fees and books which allowed her to study part-time in the evenings, while she continued to work during the day. First she took the school leaving qualification, the Bachillerato, then enrolled at the Escuela Normal de Maestras in Murcia to become a primary school teacher. Her own account of this initiative modestly indicates that she did it partly because her literary friends, one in particular, 'no *comprendía* que yo no supiera cosas'.[28] She could not, of course, go further afield, to Madrid or Paris, for example, because, unlike the majority of successful young poets writing at the time, poets such as Federico García Lorca, she did not have a family which could afford to support her in her literary endeavours and in furthering her education. In her very early years, she was restricted to a small, regional circle of writers and, up to 1926, to what she termed an autodidact's education.

However, in March 1927, she met the poet Antonio Oliver Belmás, four years her senior, also a native of Cartagena and the scion of a well-off, middle-class family. They promptly became engaged. She describes, affectionately and in the third person, their meeting and the effect he had, not just on her emotions but also on her political awareness, and indeed on the views of her parents:

> Lo cierto es que cuando se encontró con quien sería su marido más tarde, dejó cuanto quería, pensaba y hacía para adoptar la ideología de él, muchacho de muy buena familia monárquica ferviente que quizá por el ansia de ser diferente que padecen los jóvenes, pensaba de otra manera [...] Un día, sin saberlo apenas, se encontró convencida de que era imprescindible un cambio político que instaurara una República democrática. No se asombró de que sus padres se manifestaran de acuerdo (siendo profundamente cristianos y católicos, como ella aprendió a serlo desde muy chiquitita) y que además, confesaran que les parecía inevitable la caída del régimen monárquico.[29]

At that time, Oliver was associated with the group of poets who became known as the Generation of 1927 and was, among other things, editor of the literary magazine, *Verso y prosa*, which was produced in Cartagena. At this early stage in her writing life, Oliver acted as literary mentor to

[28] 'Prólogo' to *Ansia de la gracia* in *Obra poética* (1979), p. 244.
[29] *Por el camino*, I, p. 87.

14

Conde, suggesting which contemporary poets she should read, offering criticism on her writing and generally helping to pave the way for her as a poet. Up to then, she had been concentrating more on prose, and most of her reading consisted of nineteenth-century novels: 'hasta 1927, mi vocación se veía tristemente sujeta a su información decimonónica novelística'.[30] From here on, she began to read the poets and novelists of the moment, most importantly, as with all the young poets of the time, she read Juan Ramón Jiménez. In her case, this awoke 'una vena lírica de mi espíritu, inédita hasta entonces'; and she also found in the work of her fellow Levantine, the novelist Gabriel Miró, 'la común mediterraneidad, gloriosa en él'. She corresponded with both these writers. Juan Ramón took a special interest in her, publishing her poetry in his magazines *Ley: (entregas de capricho)* and *Obra en marcha: diario poético*. In 1929, her first book of poetry, *Brocal*, was published and shortly after she went to Madrid to meet Juan Ramón and his wife, Zenobia Camprubí, and Gabriel Miró.

She completed her studies and graduated as a primary teacher in 1930 and married Oliver on 5 December 1931. After her marriage, she decided to dedicate herself entirely to developing the style of prose poetry she had published in *Brocal*. She recounts that this decision to give up writing articles and stories for the newspapers and illustrated magazines had severe financial consequences. In the same breath, she acknowledges, with no little pride, that she had chosen a very difficult form of poetry and that her work was more than well regarded by a majority of critics:

> Iba yo bajo el Signo de la Poesía más absorbente. Voluntaria—y con desastre financiero para mis necesidades humanas—me negué a publicar más cuentos ni artículos en revistas ilustradas y diarios. Toda me entregué al poema en prosa, temido y temible al parecer, pero que a mí me gustaba y que me elogiaba sin tasa la crítica.[31]

In October 1933, she gave birth, after a long and difficult induced labour, to a stillborn baby girl, María del Mar. She had no further children. At this point, after fewer than two years of marriage, her intimate relationship with Oliver was under strain. Addressing her husband in a poem, unpublished in her lifetime, written shortly before she gave birth on 5 October 1933 she explains how the expected baby might somehow bring both of them redress:

---

[30] 'Prólogo' to *Ansia de la gracia* in *Obra poética* (1979), p. 244.
[31] 'Prólogo' to *Ansia de la gracia* in *Obra poética* (1979), p. 246.

Ese todo que en mí buscaste, sufriendo
y ese todo que no te pude dar nunca,
van a juntarse en el que esperamos.
Para hacer de él, yo así lo creo,
un algo que no alcanzaremos del todo:
que será la suma de lo nuestro
jamás llegado a unir.[32]

Emilió Miró observes how 'fuerte y apasionada', Conde 'vivió como una derrota su malograda maternidad', citing her despairing description of her womb post-partum as 'pobre, humillado, fracasado y dolorido'.[33] He also records that this great loss marked an end to her marriage, in all but the legal sense.

In December 1933, Conde returned to work as a primary school teacher in the Escuela Nacional de Párvulos (a primary school for orphans) in El Retén, Cartagena, where, in 1930, she had worked as an auxiliary on graduation from the Escuela Normal de Albacete as a primary teacher. In September 1934, she was appointed Inspectora-Celadora de Estudios (a teacher/house mistress) at the state orphanage of El Pardo, outside Madrid. She resigned in August of the following year due to long-standing difficulties with the right-wing CEDA-dominated local government. The culmination of this appears to have been her refusal to write a favourable article on the president of the Patronato of El Pardo for the respected liberal Madrid newspaper, *El Sol*, after which she was suspended and then sacked. Her recollections of this time on the outskirts of Madrid are sombre. Though she did go into the city from time to time and, while she was there, made the most of the opportunities the city and the society of other literary women offered, she states that otherwise 'jamás estuve más sola ni más triste', unsurprisingly as she was still mourning the loss of her daughter and any future maternity, as well as her recently deceased father.[34] She and Oliver returned to Cartagena in the wake of this experience, he for reasons of health, and took up their old lives. Her second collection of poetry in prose, *Júbilos: poemas de niños, rosas, animales, máquinas y vientos* was published in 1934, with illustrations by Norah Borges de Torre, the painter (and sister of the Argentine writer, Jorge Luis Borges), and a preface by the Chilean poet Gabriela Mistral. Mistral, it appears, had insisted that the book be published that year, even though

[32] Cited in Emilio Miró, 'La pasión o la vida', in Díez de Revenga, *Carmen Conde: voluntad creadora*, pp. 131–145, p. 137.
[33] Miró, 'La pasión o la vida', p. 137.
[34] 'Prólogo' to *Ansia de la gracia* in *Obra poética* (1979), pp. 246–47.

Conde was not certain it was quite ready, describing it as 'sin terminar a mi satisfacción'.[35] In March 1936, a mark of Conde's standing in the literary world of the time, *Júbilos* was put on the state primary school syllabus.[36]

From before their marriage Conde and Oliver had worked together to set up the Universidad Popular de Cartagena, with a mission to provide education for working-class adults for whom access to education had been a practical and financial impossibility. The institution was primarily a centre for the diffusion of culture. Among its facilities were libraries for adults and children and a cinema in which films deemed to be of educational or cultural value were shown. The Universidad Popular was the venue for art exhibitions, lecture series, debates, poetry readings and talks by writers. There were sessions at which material from the National Spoken Word Archive (Archivo de la Palabra) was played and discussed and it had its own bulletin, *Presencia*, which documented all these activities and provided a forum for those associated with the institution. Among the left-wing great and good who took part in the events organised by the Universidad Popular were the socialist Margarita Nelken and the poet Miguel Hernández, who became a close friend of the couple. Invitations were also extended to those whose political beliefs were rather more conservative. They too accepted with alacrity.

Conde and Oliver also took part in *Misiones pedagógicas*, educational workshops and classes organised in the Cartagena area under the auspices of the Patronato de Misiones Pedagógicas, a government organisation set up in 1931 dedicated to the expansion of education and culture among the rural poor. The type of activity organised under the *Misiones* programmes ranged from art exhibitions, theatre and classical music performances and poetry readings, to classes on politics and civic responsibility. The Misiones also established an effective network of small libraries in rural locations.[37]

These enterprises, the setting up of the Universidad Popular in Cartagena included, were undeniably high-minded enterprises undertaken by young, mainly liberal-minded and middle-class, writers, artists and musicians who were delighted, under the Second Republic, to be part of such an idealistic programme of events. Perhaps the best-known of these initiatives was Federico García Lorca's *La barraca* theatre troupe which

---

[35] 'Prólogo' to *Ansia de la gracia* in *Obra poética* (1979), p. 246.
[36] Fernández Hernández, 'Cronología', p. 59.
[37] See Christopher Cobb, 'The Republican State and Mass Educational-Cultural Initiatives', in *Spanish Cultural Studies*, pp. 133–138.

17

brought performances of Spanish Golden Age drama to rural villages during this period. However, there was frequently a considerable mismatch between the intentions and enthusiasm of the middle-class literati and the poor, rural farm labourers and their families who would have welcomed simple food aid in the place of high-flown lectures from well-meaning city folk. As the playwright Alejandro Casona noted: 'they needed bread and medicine and we had only songs and poems in our bags'.[38] Later, writing about herself in the third person, Conde was to spell out her own apolitical idealism in response to the Franco regime's condemnation of her work for the Republic during and before the Civil War:

> ... ella no pertenecía a ningún partido, no era militante de nada, solamente escritora fundadora con su novio entonces luego marido, de la Universidad Popular de Cartagena ajenísima a cuanto no significara estrictamente cultura y que operaba dentro de la máxima convivencia humana y social.[39]

At the outbreak of war, in July 1936, Conde had to turn down the opportunity for a study trip to France and Belgium to examine popular education initiatives in these countries, for which she had been awarded a grant and which she should have taken up that very month. Antonio Oliver, who, in tandem with all his other activities, had been a full-time Posts and Telegraphs civil servant since 1922, in spite of recurrent bouts of poor health, joined Radio Frente Popular No. 2 as a propaganda official and spent the war in various postings throughout Andalucía.

During this time, on a personal level, as she began to form friendships within the group of women writers and artists who frequented the feminist Lyceum Club in Madrid in the early 1930s, which she was able to visit from time to time, Conde evolved from being the self-taught, provincial neophyte Antonio Oliver had taken under his literary as well as amorous wing in 1927 into a woman who understood that she would never be able to give of herself 'ese todo que no te pude dar nunca' within a traditional marriage.[40] Instead, the encounter of her life took place in February 1936 when she made the acquaintance of Amanda Junquera, 'ser extraordinario, delicada escritora'.[41] Junquera's husband, Cayetano

[38] Quoted in Cobb, 'The Republican State', p. 136.
[39] Carmen Conde, *Por el camino*, I, p. 93.
[40] See Ferris, *Carmen Conde: Vida, pasión y verso de una escritora olvidada*, pp. 387–472. This is the first study to foreground Conde's relationship with Amanda Junquera.
[41] Susana March, who met her with Carmen Conde and Cayetano Alcázar in 1949, provides this description in Susana March, 'Prólogo' in *El tiempo es un río lentísimo de fuego* (Barcelona: Ediciones 29, 1978), pp. 9–10, p. 9.

Alcázar, a political conservative, held the chair of Spanish History at the University of Murcia and was one of those political conservatives happy to become involved with the Universidad Popular de Cartagena. Though each in her way would remain loyal to her husband, the two women would never again be completely parted. Although it would be facile to suggest that after the war, in Franco's Spain, they had no alternative but to remain, at least on the surface, married, particularly Junquera whose husband's position under the Franco administration, from 1945 as Director-General of Universities, rendered any scandal unthinkable, the lived truth is probably considerably more complex and, almost certainly, more compassionate on all sides. What is incontestable is that Junquera became Conde's muse and protector, in equal part, for the rest of her life. Twenty years after they first met, on 23 November 1956, Conde inscribed the following words on a handwritten copy of the first edition of *Mujer sin Edén* (1947) which she had confected, painstakingly, for her lover:

Amanda,
　　he copiado para ti, en el transcurso de años, poema a poema, este libro (de su primera edición) que hice en tu casa ya a tu lado. Cada palabra lleva tu recuerdo y tu cariño. Lo sabes, pero yo te lo digo también desde aquí.
Carmen.[42]

Months after this monumental encounter, the war broke out and cast everything into confusion. In many ways, it offered Conde and Juquera opportunities early on in their relationship they might not otherwise have had. Conde followed Oliver to his posting in Guadix but soon returned to Cartagena when her mother fell ill. In November 1936, she and her mother moved to Murcia when the bombardment of Cartagena became too severe. While there, she worked as an interim teacher in a primary school and gave classes to illiterate adults in the Casa de la Mujer of the Agrupación de Mujeres Antifascistas. She rejoined her husband for brief periods in Jaén, Úbeda and Baeza, spending, from 1937 on, most of her time in Valencia. Alcázar had been transferred to a chair there in Autumn 1937, as it was the only university still functioning, and Junquera went with him. Conde and Junquera both enrolled in the Facultad de Letras at the university of Valencia to study Spanish literature in 1937. Later on, in 1938, both successfully sat *oposiciones* to become librarians though neither was subsequently in a position to take up a post. In 1938, Alcázar

---

[42] Reproduced in Miró, 'La pasión o la vida', p. 140.

was seconded to the Department of Information in Baza, where by then, coincidentally, Oliver was also stationed. Conde and Junquera briefly rejoined their husbands in Baza and spent the rest of the war in Valencia.

In 1939, just as the war was coming to a close, Conde and Oliver could have left their homeland, had they wished. However, unlike the vast majority of writers, artists and intellectuals associated with the Republican cause, they decided to remain. Though Junquera's position and her loyalty to her own widowed mother must have been crucial factors in Conde's decision-making process at the time, the explanation she chose to provide in an interview she gave at the age of 77 strikes a wholly justifiable air of nobility:

> Mi marido me dijo «no he hecho más que defender mis ideas y a mi patria, así que no me voy; no creo que nos maten, y si nos vamos todos este tío (por Franco) se quedará nada más que con los suyos». Y así nos quedamos, pero cómo lo pasamos ...[43]

Oliver was imprisoned in Baza at the end of the war. Conde would have been incarcerated as well but she was spirited away from Valencia as soon as the Republican government surrendered and hidden in the Junquera family flat in Madrid between 1939 and 1940. Then, she and Junquera moved to rented houses in San Lorenzo de El Escorial, outside Madrid, and returned to Madrid in the autumn of 1941 where they rented a flat in the Calle Wellingtonia. They remained there until 1945, in a building belonging to the poet Vicente Aleixandre, who himself lived on the ground floor.

Both Conde and Oliver had to stand trial for their activities during the war. While Conde was in hiding in Madrid, her mother lived under the protection of a teacher at the Conservatory of Music in Murcia, an old family friend who herself received threats because Conde's mother was in her house. Conde appeared before three military councils and was ultimately, in 1944, allowed to go free because of lack of evidence. Oliver was almost immediately sentenced to a long term of imprisonment but eventually released thanks to the influence of his brother, a staunch Nationalist.[44] He then remained, until 1945, in his sister's house in Murcia, keeping his identity hidden. Deprived of his government post and with most of his former publishing contacts closed to him, he was obliged to work for the next few years for his brother-in-law, an architect and builder,

[43] *Por el camino*, III, p. 267.
[44] *Por el camino*, I, p. 207.

often in a form of physical labour which constituted more than a mere indignity to a man with a congenital heart condition. In Conde's opinion, his was by far the worse experience, and she condemns the boorish and ungrateful behaviour of this brother-in-law who was so quick to forget the support and protection she had afforded him when his house was under threat under the Republic:

> El obligado enclaustramiento [...] fue muy malo para mi marido, a causa de su cuñado precisamente, hombre oscuro y pedante cargado de ingratitud ya que su vida y su casa (como tantas otras) fueron defendidas y protegidas por nuestros nombres, yéndome yo con mi madre junto a mi cuñada respaldando a su absurdo marido ante los políticos de la región y sus colaboradores.[45]

Conde and Oliver thus lived apart until 1945 when he was finally in a position to live openly in Madrid. They then resided, together with her mother, who also left Murcia for Madrid, at the Pensión Valls on the Calle Goya until 1949 when they definitively established themselves in a flat on the Calle Ferraz. His health, never robust, was permanently weakened after the privations of these years and thus the burden of keeping her mother, her husband and herself fell more fully onto Conde's shoulders. She recalls that after the war: 'mi marido era un hombre muy enfermo y yo no quería que trabajara más allá de lo que sus fuerzas le permitían'.[46]

In the introduction to a series of reflections written while living with Junquera in San Lorenzo de El Escorial, Conde attributes her own survival during this period to the friendships and contacts she and her husband maintained with Nationalist supporters and to her own determination, already mentioned, to protect her own Nationalist-inclined friends and family from attack under the Republic and within the Republican zone during the war itself. After the Republican capitulation, she explains how, as distinct from the official attitude of the victorious regime, these individual friends and associates made a point of differentiating between the conduct of those adhering to profoundly held political beliefs and those opportunists who committed crimes under cover of the Republic:

> ... tanto mi marido como yo habíamos defendido incruentamente nuestras ideas, si legales antes del 18 de julio de 1936, ilegales ante el pronunciamiento militar que [...] llegaba a nombrarnos como auxiliares de la rebelión. Y ¿quiénes se habían rebelado: ellos o nosotros? [...] la hostilidad triunfante no hacía distingos entre los autores de hechos criminales y los pensamientos

[45] *Por el camino*, I, p. 208.
[46] *Por el camino*, III, p. 258.

de los intelectuales afectos a la República que vino sin sangre de nadie [...

La confianza en nuestra actuación pasada que, por muy republicana que hubiera sido siempre fue decente y lógica, nos ayudaba bastante al tratar de sobrevivir con la ayuda de amigos que nos conocían y por ello creían en nosotros, a ciegas si vale decir esto. Dios les bendiga siempre.[47]

In that first year in the Junquera household in Madrid, her existence was so completely clandestine that the porter in her building, who was obliged by law to declare all those resident in his block 'a fin de que no se escapara ninguno sin llevarse su merecido' omitted her from his list. For their part, the Junquera family routinely suggested to those of their callers and habitués who had met Conde during the war that she had gone to (Latin) America while she herself listened, with some sense of bitter irony at her own and her husband's final act of idealism, from her 'habitación-refugio':

Los amigos de la casa que me conocieron en guerra solían preguntar por mí. Les oía desde la habitación-refugio en que me encontraba y también las forzosas respuestas: «Creemos que se fue a América», decían vagamente ...

Aquello hubiere sido lo mejor que podíamos haber hecho, pero lo rechazamos mi marido y yo porque nos horrorizaba la expatriación. Preferíamos aguantar lo inevitable y mantenernos con dignidad en nuestra Patria.[48]

At the end of the series of reflections or *notas* she wrote during her time in El Escorial, she reiterates her thanks to her protectors and friends. In a comment in which she remarks upon her own deliberate exclusion of any reference to the war and its consequences from these reflections, she draws a wry parallel between this self-censorship and her condition of 'internal exile'. In the words of Ernesto Giménez Caballero himself, who championed a match between Pilar Primo de Rivera and Hitler and was an acquaintance of hers, this was a period of 'excedencia' (in normal circumstances, leave granted when a member of staff is deemed surplus to requirements):

Se prescinde en ellas [ las notas] de toda referencia al desastre que, en lo familiar, obligó a una «excedencia» de la sociedad que ya vivía su aire vencedor [...]; voluntariamente exentas [las notas] de traumas y explicitaciones. Sin embargo, hay nombres tan queridos de quienes facilitaron y protegieron mi exilio interior. Inolvidables serán hasta el fin de mis días. Me dieron paz física, comprensión, tolerancia [...] Que Dios bendiga a mis protectores y mantenga mi gratitud.[49]

[47] *Por el camino*, I, pp. 207–208.
[48] *Por el camino*, I, pp. 207–208.
[49] *Por el camino*, I, p. 271. She speaks of Giménez Caballero as an *amigo superficial*, although before the war he had been a significant figure whose patronage she would have been glad to have. See Ferris, *Carmen Conde: Vida, pasión y verso*, p. 377.

It is important to note, that although Conde became, under Oliver's tutelage, a convinced adherent of Republican ideals and then a loyal servant of the Republic, above all in matters cultural and educational, and would have realised through her relationship with Junquera and her association with other progressive women writers that her own faith was by then far from orthodox, she never for a moment considered renouncing her Catholic heritage nor did she succumb to pressure to align herself in any way with the strong anti-clerical ethos in the Republican zone during the war. When she was denounced, as late as 1949, as a Marxist, even her enemies were obliged to regard the accusation with incredulity, so much so perhaps that, in that same year, she was finally granted a passport.[50]

In fact, Catholic spirituality never ceased to be integral to her work. She tells a touchingly ingenuous story of how she believed, in her early teens, as an adolescent writer starting off, that Santa Teresa, no mean exponent herself, might be called upon for writerly inspiration:

> [...] era tal mi fervor literario y místico, que coloqué una estampa de Santa Teresa de Jesús encima de la minúscula mesita donde escribía en mis veladas secretas. Santa Teresa estaba acompañada del Espíritu Santo, que le *dictaba*. ¡Cómo le pedí yo la gracia de su soplo! Estuve convencida durante mucho tiempo de que la Santa tendría para mí una sonrisa de protección.[51]

As an adult, her attitude to religious practice naturally became comparatively relaxed: 'soy una mujer católica [...] claro, no me paso la vida en las novenas, porque eso ya lo hice con mi madre en mi juventud y salí atracada de todo eso'.[52] However, it seems clear that her adolescent identification of Santa Teresa as a role model for her own writing was not merely due to the ubiquity of Santa Teresa as a figure of veneration for little girls; rather it was evidence of an early and deep-rooted instinct that mysticism would prove to be fundamental to her own work. It is abundantly clear from her post-Civil War poetry, from *Ansia de la gracia* (1945) onwards, that her engagement with matters religious takes place on a spiritual and mystical plane. Miró asserts that this vein of profound mysticism and cosmic vision in her adult poetry has its roots in *Mientras los hombres mueren*, observing that the much-lauded *Mujer sin Edén* (1947)

> ... es hija de un tiempo sombrío, es inseparable de tanta sangre, derramada, de tanto desprecio del hombre por el hombre. Continuación, por tanto, de

---

[50] *Por el camino*, III, p. 258.
[51] 'Prólogo' to *Ansia de la gracia* in *Obra poética* (1979), p. 243.
[52] *Por el camino*, III, p. 258.

*Mientras los hombres mueren*, y en cierto modo, culminación de un decenio fecundísimo de creatividad de su autora. Las imagenes y metáforas cósmicas, recurrentes en toda su obra, se empapan en *Mujer sin Edén* de resonancias bíblicas ...[53]

While these were years of intense poetic productivity, they were also economically and socially difficult for Conde and Oliver. During the 1940s, they published poetry, very discreetly and with difficulty, under their own names and produced what might be termed journeyman literature using noms de plume: in her case, children's literature, biographies, history, hagiographies, novels and stories, which she wrote as Florentina del Mar and Magdalena Noguera, among others. With Alcázar's help, in 1945 she obtained a post in the registry secretariat at the University of Madrid; later she was moved to the publications department. She worked at the same time at the Consejo Superior de Investigaciones Científicas, as editor of the *Boletín bibliográfico*, and subsequently worked there until her retirement in 1971. Her tactic in the 1940s and 1950s was not to seek out prestigious posts and not to attract attention to herself, but to make a living and to dedicate as much time as possible to her writing.[54]

In this way, once her passport was returned to her, she travelled freely from the 1950s onwards, mostly in Europe. She and Oliver went on a tour of Central America in 1963, in connection with their acquisition of the Ruben Darío Archive, of which Oliver became the first director, under state auspices, in 1956. In 1967, she was awarded the prestigious Premio Nacional de Poesía for her *Obra poética*, edited by Emilio Miró. Antonio Oliver died the following year and, in accordance with his wishes, she brought out his *Obras completas* in 1971. Her subsequent collection, *A este lado de la eternidad* (1970) is permeated by Oliver's absence, reflections on death and on the life they had shared together, in one way or another, over a period of forty years. Their relationship is marked in particular in the elegiac 'Réquiem por nosotros dos', in which she vindicates the integrity of their love:

> Yo te quise, tu amor se salva intacto
> de todos los fragores de la vida.
> Me quisiste también, estoy segura
> de que nada quebró lo que fue nuestro.[55]

[53] Miró, 'La pasión o la vida', p. 145.
[54] *Por el camino*, III, p. 257.
[55] Miró, *Poesía completa*, p. 698.

24

Cayetano Alcázar had died ten years previously, in 1958. With her customary determination to honour debts and loyalties owed, Conde composed an elegy for him too, lamenting him as 'amigo de los años más difíciles/ de los muchos sencillos días nuestros'.[56] After Oliver's death, she and Junquera lived together in Junquera's family residence, until the latter's death, from Alzheimer's disease, in 1986. From the mid-1980s onwards, the symptoms of Alzheimer's became perceptible in Conde also, though this did not stop her continuing to work and give interviews throughout that decade. In 1992, she moved into a care home in Majadahonda, north west of Madrid and died, 'cuando ya su mente llevaba un tiempo extraviada en las nieblas de Alzheimer', on 8 January 1996.[57]

In 1978, Conde became the first woman elected to the Spanish Royal Academy, an institution founded in 1713 by the Marqués de Villena and a group of equally learned men with the express intention, as with all the other academies founded in Western Europe during the Enlightenment, of preserving the integrity of the national language and its culture. On the death of the playwright Miguel Mihura in 1977, seat K became vacant. Before Carmen Conde, the only woman to have been elected to the Spanish Royal Academy was María Isidra Quintina de Guzmán y de la Cerda, the countess of Paredes. She was elected to the Royal Academy at the age of seventeen in 1784 by order of the king, Carlos III, who professed himself astonished by her knowledge of science, literature and the Latin, Greek, French and Italian languages.[58] After giving her inaugural address on 28 September 1784, she took no further part in the activities of the Academy.[59] Until 1978, when Carmen Conde was nominated, no other woman was welcomed into the Academy.

In 1978, feminist commentators in the Spanish press were scathing in their condemnation of the Academy's history of overt misogyny even though the Academy had, for the first time in its history, made the grand gesture of sanctioning an all-female shortlist and thus assuring the election of a woman. Josefina Carabias, for example, in an interview with

[56] Miró, *Poesía completa*, p. 667; *Réquiem por Cayetano* (Madrid: Edición no venal de la autora, 1958).

[57] See Ángel L. Prieto de Paula, 'Carmen Conde, la primera mujer', *El País*, 11 August 2007.

[58] José Luis Ferris, 'Del olvido al fervor popular: una mujer en la Academia (1978– 1979)', in *Carmen Conde: Voluntad creadora*, pp. 179–195, p. 182.

[59] See Pilar Nieva de la Paz, 'Una polémica politico-literaria en torno a la incorporación de la mujer a la Real Academia Española (1978): ¿Rosa Chacel o Carmen Conde?', *Voz y letra*. XV, 2, 2004, pp. 105–113, p. 106.

the then director of the Academy, the poet Dámaso Alonso, includes an anecdote about the scandalous exclusion of Emilia Pardo Bazán, one of the towering figures, without exception, of nineteenth-century literature in Castilian. The aggressively ironic tone of her writing encapsulates a level of anger and frustration among cultured women over the exclusion of female writers and intellectuals which had been building since the Academy's rejection of the lexicographer María Moliner in 1972:

> ... a ninguno se le ocurriría emplear los argumentos que empleó don Juan Valera cuando se trató de la candidatura de la condesa de Pardo Bazán— que no llegó ni a poder sentarse—en el sentido de que «la presencia de una mujer entre los académicos sería un enredo, una perturbación, además les impediría hablar con libertad y contar chistes verdes», a los que, por lo visto, era muy aficionado [...] Claro que, a lo de los «cuentos verdes», doña Emilia, gallega zumbona, respondió que «por eso no se preocupasen, puesto que ella también podía contar algunos muy buenos».[60]

Carabias' disgust at the puerility exhibited in Valera's day (Pardo Bazán was turned down by the Academy three times, the last in 1912, while Concepción Arenal and Gertrudis Gómez de Avellaneda, whose candidacy she promoted, were also rejected) is mixed with a high degree of scepticism at the Academy's apparent final capitulation. The move to facilitate the election of a woman in 1978 was seen by many commentators on the left as hypocritical at worst and opportunist at best.[61]

Very early on, news was leaked that the election would principally be between Carmen Conde and Rosa Chacel. The third candidate, Carmen Guirao, a distinguished medical doctor, was seen from the outset as an outsider. The battle lines were drawn from the start. In the right-wing press, Carmen Conde was represented as the candidate of the right and a writer whose work exemplified the 'acceptable' feminine qualities of passion, eroticism, idealism, emotion, feeling and closeness to nature while it was argued that Rosa Chacel's literary output embodied distance, intellectual coldness and formal difficulty.[62] In the left-wing press, Conde's political credentials were questioned, though the merit of her work was never placed in doubt:

> Rosa Chacel es el exilio—su literatura, incuestionada—, y Carmen Conde— tampoco cuestionada su obra—, queda para la disputa de los subsectores como perteneciente al exilio interior o no ...[63]

[60] Quoted in Ferris, 'Del olvido al fervor popular', p. 186.
[61] Ferris, 'Del olvido al fervor popular', p. 182.
[62] See Nieva de la Paz, 'Una polémica politico-literaria', pp. 109–110.
[63] Ferris, 'Del olvido al fervor popular', p. 186.

This element of doubt over the validity of Carmen Conde's internal exile is understandable. Never an easy or emollient personality, she expected to be taken at her word, however complex or apparently contradictory her behaviour or given opinion might appear to be. Neither could hers be described as a pure form of internal exile. She was sheltered and advised during the difficult first decade of the dictatorship by friends within the Franco regime, and, for the duration of the dictatorship, she eschewed overt political comment or activism within Spain. She also maintained, stubbornly and openly, friendships on both sides of the political divide. As her long-time secretary, and granddaughter of Rubén Darío, the journalist Rosa Villacastín, avers: 'Era una mujer muy dura, seca a veces, pero tenía una parte muy entrañable [...] a la hora de la amistad, se olvidaba de las ideologías, y lo mismo era amiga de Tierno Galván que de Manuel Fraga o Luis Rosales.'[64]

She did publish one major statement of defiance, during the dictatorship. *En un mundo de fugitivos* came out in Buenos Aires in 1960. While a significant proportion of its content poured excoriating scorn on the Franco regime, because of censorship and the limited readership for poetry, it did not have an impact in Spain at the time. One third of the collection is devoted to overtly political poems, written over a twenty-year period, from the immediate aftermath of the Civil War onwards. Seven years later, the censorship environment had changed so much that it became possible to include it, a little miracle in itself, in Emilio Miró's prize-winning anthology, *Obra poética,* where it appears, again, to have passed relatively unnoticed.[65] Thus, neither the contribution she made in this collection nor that in *Mientras los hombres mueren* did much to counteract the general perception which had built up by the late 1970s

[64] Remarks made at the launch of Ferris's biography of Conde, on 19 June 2007, in the Café Gijón, Madrid. 'Ferris rescata en una biografía la figura olvidada de [la] escritora Carmen Conde', 19 June 2007, www.Terra.es. Enrique Tierno Galván (1918–86) was an anti-Franco intellectual. Forced out of his Salamanca university chair in 1965 and into exile, he was reinstated in 1976 and became the PSOE mayor of Madrid from 1979 to 1986. Manuel Fraga (1922–), the great political survivor of the Franco era, was Minister of Information and Tourism (1962–69) and is credited with the more relaxed attitude of the regime towards cultural matters and censorship during the 1960s. In the 1980s he led the opposition to the PSOE government and from 1990–2005, he was president of the Xunta de Galicia. Luis Rosales (1910–1992), a member of the Generation of 1927, was the poet laureate of the Nationalists during the Civil War though he moderated his politics as he grew older. He was elected to the Spanish Royal Academy in 1962.

[65] *En un mundo de fugitivos* (Buenos Aires: Losada, 1960).

that she had been a fellow traveller of the regime, a 'conformista'.[66]

Her own musings on the debate in the press over her candidacy for seat K show exasperation at the recurrent and facile misprision of her behaviour and political beliefs. As a result of this, she appears to have believed her chances of election to be remote:

> *Jueves 2 de febrero.* En *Ya* vienen dos páginas con las «académicas» *in pectore*.[67] Y en lo que se dice de Rosa Chacel la da ya como ocupante del sillón «K». Me llama la mujer de Eugenio Montes [an academician] para darme la seguridad del voto de su marido y me habla mal de Rosa Chacel, la «exiliada de izquierdas», como dicen los suyos, y yo ¡DE DERECHAS!

> *Sábado 4 de febrero.* Me llama a las 10,30 desde Barcelona Guillermo Díaz-Plaja muy animoso. «¡Tenemos que hacer los discursos! Tiene que ganar quien aguantó aquí 40 años a pie firme». En fin, ya veremos, yo no pongo la menor esperanza.

> *Jueves 9 de febrero.* Jueves resolutorio. Los académicos entre Rosa Chacel y yo. Exilio voluntario y 40 años de aguante con dignidad y valor y obra ...[68]

In the end and against her own expectations, Guillermo Díaz-Plaja formally welcomed Carmen Conde into the Real Academia Española as its first woman member in almost two centuries. During her tenure, she kept faith with women writers and championed the successful candidacy of the novelist Elena Quiroga in 1982. When Conde died, her chair was taken by another woman novelist, Ana María Matute.[69]

Her inaugural address, *Poesía ante el tiempo y la inmortalidad*, delivered on 28 January 1979, opens with an outright condemnation of the Academy's reluctance to honour great female writers. She declares it to be unjust and antiquated:

> Mis primeras palabras son de agradecimiento a vuestra generosidad al elegirme para un puesto que, secularmente, no se concedió a ninguna de

---

[66] Guillermo Díaz-Plaja makes special mention of both collections in his official response to her inaugural address to the Royal Academy. See Guillermo Díaz-Plaja, 'Discurso' in Carmen Conde, *Poesía ante el tiempo y la inmortalidad* (Madrid: Real Academia Española, 1979), pp. 55–76, pp. 64–65, p. 72.

[67] *In pectore*, Latin for in one's breast, usually used in the Catholic Church to denote the holder of an office who must, for whatever reason, keep the matter secret. For example, it is believed that Pope John Paul II appointed at least one cardinal *in pectore* towards the end of his papacy. That cardinal, if he exists, has not disclosed that he holds such an office. Carmen Conde's use of it here probably refers more to the fact that the candidates are aware of their nomination.

[68] Ferris, 'Del olvido al fervor popular', p.188.

[69] Nieva de la Paz, 'Una polémica politico-literaria', p. 112.

nuestras grandes escritoras ya desaparecidas. Permitid que también manifieste mi homenaje de admiración y respeto a sus obras. Vuestra noble decisión pone fin a una tan injusta como vetusta discriminación literaria.[70]

She goes on to trace her own line of inheritance from three women poets of the nineteenth century: Gertrudis Gómez de Avellaneda, Carolina Coronado and Rosalía de Castro. She also mentions Concepción Arenal in passing. In 1979, an indication of the status of women's poetry in the literary canon, only one of these poets appears to have been available to her in print. She acknowledges, in a footnote, that she relied on photocopies supplied by Carmen Bravo-Villasante for access to the work of Coronado and Gómez de Avellaneda. This note may, to some extent, be taken as a barbed comment on the misogyny of a literary establishment which allowed this work to slip into oblivion. She defends Coronado and Gómez de Avellaneda for doing much more than conforming to the 'casi permitido esquema' of 'movimientos de ternura, [las] formas blandas y delicadas, propias de un pecho femenil'. While this properly removes their work from the nineteenth-century ghetto of themes permissible for women, it also, astutely, refutes the categorisation of her own poetry as peculiarly feminine which had been prevalent in the press before her election. In fact, her tribute to women writers paid, she goes on to cite a list, which is exclusively, one might say defiantly, male, of writers whom she believes have influenced her trajectory into time and immortality: Gustavo Adolfo Bécquer, Miguel de Unamuno, Juan Ramón Jiménez, Antonio Machado, Luis Cernuda, Salvador Espriu, Juan Maragall and her husband, Antonio Oliver Belmás.

Yet, in her own early years, Carmen Conde benefited from the friendship and support of important women writers and literary figures, notably Gabriela Mistral, who was, in the 1930s, the Chilean consul in Lisbon, and of course, the redoubtable Zenobia Camprubí, whose husband, Juan Ramón Jiménez, championed her work until he and Zenobia left for Puerto Rico in 1936. She also developed an intense, perhaps passionate, friendship with her renowned contemporary and member of the Generation of 1927, Ernestina de Champourcín, with whom she first began to correspond in 1927, and she was close to the poet Concha Méndez and the philosopher María Zambrano.[71] She was, therefore, an integral part of

---

[70] Carmen Conde, *Poesía ante el tiempo y la inmortalidad*, pp. 9–51, p. 9.
[71] Fernández Hernández, 'Cronología' in *Carmen Conde: Voluntad creadora*, p. 58; Ferris, *Carmen Conde: Vida, pasión y verso*, pp. 319–386.

what might be considered a network of women writers and artists during the 1930s, many of whom were prominently involved in the cultural and educational initiatives of the Second Republic.

From the 1940s on, she herself became a senior figure, not least because most of her own contemporaries had gone into exile. In her prologue to the first collection Conde published after her nomination to the Academy, *El tiempo es un río lentísimo de fuego,* the poet Susana March pays handsome tribute to her contribution to women's poetry in Spain since the Civil War:

> Creo que Carmen Conde es la Madre de todas las mujeres que han escrito versos a partir de los años cuarenta. Ella, tan materna siempre, atendiéndonos a todas, publicando críticas y libros y antologías sobre todas, ¡con una generosidad tan difícil de encontrar en nuestra profesión! Ella, dándose siempre a sus compañeras, aconsejando, comprendiendo, ayudando ...[72]

The last word on this might be left to Dolores Ibárruri, La Pasionaria. It was one of Conde's great regrets that she destroyed the photos and the short film she had made of La Pasionaria's visit to Valencia during the war. She explains that she did this when she was in hiding in Madrid in order not to place the Junquera family in any more danger than necessary. The redoubtable Ibárruri, on hearing the female governor of Murcia's comments on Conde's lack of orthodox revolutionary zeal, replied with a stout defence of the right of the poet to her individual voice:

> Deja tú en paz a Carmen, que ella tiene su propia línea en su poesía y no precisa de la nuestra.[73]

Perhaps that might be a sentiment applicable to the whole of Conde's creative life, full of apparent contradiction on the surface, anchored in absolute integrity beneath.

### Mientras los hombres mueren

Carmen Conde's heyday as a poet was undoubtedly in the thirty years between 1939 and 1971, a trajectory which can be traced from *Ansia de la gracia* (1945) and *Mujer sin Edén* (1947) to *Derribado arcángel* (1960) and *En un mundo de fugitivos* (1960) to *A este lado de la eternidad* (1970). Her poetry is a profoundly passionate, complex and sensory exploration of the contradictions of human existence and of what it is, especially, to be

---

[72] Susana March, 'Prólogo', p. 9.
[73] *Por el camino*, I, pp. 118–119. This recollection is dated 15 May 1974.

a woman alone and buffeted between the emptiness of the cosmic infinite and the storms of human passion. As Emilio Miró observes:

> Esa tensión entre contrarios, eterno conflicto humano entre la luz y las tinieblas, es el eje de la fuerza motriz de la escritura en prosa—en verso, sobre todo—de Carmen Conde, río caudaloso—sereno y limpio, a veces, proceloso y turbio, las más—, expresión intensísima de su propia, apasionada existencia.[74]

Turbulence more often than serenity, a preoccupation with the place of humanity in the cosmos, in nature, the signal importance of love, the course of destiny, these, the major currents of the poetry of her maturity, are also prefigured in *Mientras los hombres mueren*.

*Mientras los hombres mueren* diverges radically from the gentle, lyrical vignettes of nature, childhood and young love she offered in her two previous collections of prose poetry. She employs the techniques of the poets of the Generation of 1927, the piling of image upon image, reference upon reference in a direct engagement with the awful, material reality of war. She depicts a nightmarish world where dream merges with reality and images are fleeting. They are described in a kind of visual shorthand and pass almost too quickly for their relevance to be grasped. She does not try to make the language sing – as prose it has no obligation to rhyme – but she often goes out of her way to render it angular and harsh, in keeping with acerbity of the world she depicts. In sum, she makes very few concessions to her reader. The second section of *Mientras los hombres mueren*, 'A los niños muertos en la guerra', is more open and declamatory, a little closer to the rhythms of the popular ballad and the lament, but challenging nonetheless.

One way of approaching the poetry would be to look at the most famous image to emerge from the Civil War, Pablo Picasso's *Guernica*, painted in response to the bombing of the Basque town of Guernica on 26 April 1937 by the German Condor Legion and the Italian Legionary Air Force (*Aviazione Legionaria*) and exhibited in the Spanish Pavilion at the 1937 Paris Expo (World Fair) under the aegis of the Republican government. The painting follows the cubist aesthetic of packing all the narrative elements of the real-life event, the carnage at Guernica, on top of one another, in a nightmarish series of seemingly impossible juxtapositions. None of the elements are rendered in a true-to-life manner and most are represented as fragments of a whole, or depicted from unusual perspectives. There is also a deliberate absence of colour, the picture

[74] Emilio Miró, 'La pasión o la vida', p. 145.

tells its story in shades of grey, reflecting perhaps the worldwide media coverage of the atrocity and the means by which Picasso himself came to know of it, and there is very little depth of field. The viewer has to work to construct a linear narrative out of all these elements, to establish a relationship between the distorted, caricatured forms and the original reality, to weigh the impact of the form chosen by the artist on the story to which he is responding. Carmen Conde's poems in *Mientras los hombres mueren* are often similar in methodology to Picasso's *Guernica*. The reader is required to reassemble the images which come pouring out, one after another, to fill in, using logic and reference to reality, the narrative gaps which make a linear tale out of a complex series of apparently unrelated or deliberately semi-realised images, and to consider the effect this form of consciously difficult expression has in heightening the emotional and rhetorical impact of the words on the page.

Conde's imagery deals with the many ways in which she has visualised the bodies of the dead merging into the land. In her dystopian, insomniac's world, the land, the heavens and the sea react in apocalyptic terms to the catastrophe of war, erupting, collapsing, inundating the young men dying at the front and the women and children being wiped out at home. She, the poet, becomes the voice of her people, a mother or would-be mother refusing to bring another child into the world until the war ceases and encouraging all other women of child-bearing age to follow suit; a mother lamenting the children blown to smithereens by enemy bombs or shellfire in the cities and the young men, too young to have fathered their own children, returning their unspent seed to the ground as their bodies rot into it. Though others may, she cannot sleep while the world consumes itself in flames around her. She remains permanently on guard, vigilant. The enemy is sometimes brother to the young man he kills, sometimes the distant, foreign airman in the sky who has no contact with or knowledge of those he calmly annihilates on the ground. All those who die, who are mutilated or who lose loved ones are victims. At no point does she suggest that one Spaniard is better than another or more in the right than the other. Her only request is that human beings treat each other with common humanity. When it comes to the deaths of children and the impact this has on their grieving mothers, she is, as her preface attests, even more direct, even more uncompromising in her willingness to confront the awfulness. Here she also takes on the presumed indifference of the enemy airmen who rain bombs down on what to them are mere objectives on a grid.

The poetry is almost too much to bear, both in its complex and demanding mode of expression and in what it communicates, because the experience of war is almost inexpressible. Since both *Mientras los hombres mueren* and 'A los niños muertos en la guerra' come to the inevitable conclusion of the end of the war and the defeat of the Republican government, there is an identifiable trajectory, from horror through despair to resignation and the small hope that some semblance of normality might be returned if the children who have been sent away are allowed back. Yet, this must have looked like a very forlorn hope to a poet sequestered for her own protection in a room in a flat in Madrid in the winter of famine of 1939 with the Second World War about to explode all around her.

# Note on editions

This edition is primarily based on Emilio Miró's two editions of *Mientras los hombres mueren*: collected in his *Carmen Conde: Obra poética* (1967), which was prepared in collaboration with the poet, and in his *Carmen Conde: Poesía completa* (2007), which was compiled with the assistance of staff from the Patronato Carmen Conde–Antonio Oliver (Archivo Municipal de Cartagena). I consulted manuscripts held at the Patronato and I am especially indebted to Caridad Fernández Hernández for her kind assistance in making these papers available to me.

The vast majority of the poems in the two sections of *Mientras los hombres mueren*, 'Mientras los hombre mueren' and 'A los niños muertos en la guerra' are to be found in a copybook, written out in sequence, in Conde's hand. Many of the individual poems carry the dates of their composition. The title page for the collection in the copybook indicates that they were written in Valencia, 1937–39. There is no indication of precisely when Conde made this fair copy. In the 1940s and early 1950s, when her access to publication was severely limited, she used to prepare handwritten collections of her poetry, usually dedicating them to her muse, Amanda Junquera. As there is no dedication on the copybook containing *Mientras*, it is more likely this is the original manuscript produced in or around 1939 and not a subsequent copy. There are manuscript sheets for some, though not all, of the additional poems included in published version of *Mientras*.

Overall, Conde changed the poems very little between manuscript and publication. Where there are significant alterations, I have included the original passages or poems in appendices for comparison. Very occasionally, and usually because of a printing error or anomaly in one or other of the Miró editions, I have opted to revert to an orthography used in the original manuscript. I have explained these changes in the relevant commentary.

This is the first edition of *Mientras los hombres mueren* to appear as a separate volume since it was first published in Milan in 1953.

# Select bibliography

Carmen Conde's entire published output is listed in *Carmen Conde: voluntad creadora* (cited below), pp. 267–270. The following is a select bibliography of her poetry and other material relevant to this edition.

## Works by Carmen Conde

### Select poetry

*Brocal: Poemas* (Madrid: La Lectura, 1929).
*Júbilos: Poemas de niños, rosas, animales, máquinas y vientos* (Murcia: Sudeste, 1934).
*Signo de amor* (Granada: Vientos del Sur, 1945).
*Ansia de la Gracia* (Madrid: Editorial Hispánica, 1945).
*Sea la luz* (Madrid: Mensajes, 1947).
*Mi fin en el viento* (Madrid: Colección Adonais, 1947).
*Mujer sin Edén* (Madrid: Jura, 1947).
*Mientras los hombres mueren* (Milano: Istituto Editoriale Cisalpino, 1953).
*Las oscuras raíces* (Barcelona: Bruguera, 1954).
*Vivientes los siglos* (Madrid: Los Poetas, 1954).
*En un mundo de fugitivos* (Buenos Aires: Losada, 1960).
*Derribado arcángel: Poemas* (Madrid: Revista de Occidente, 1960).
*En la tierra de nadie* (Murcia: Laurel del Sureste, 1962).
*Los poemas del mar menor* (Murcia: Universidad, Cátedra «Saavedra Fájardo», 1962).
*A este lado de la eternidad* (Madrid: Biblioteca Nueva, 1970).
*Cancionero de la enamorada* (Ávila: Institución Gran Duque de Alba, 1971).
*Corrosión* (Madrid: Biblioteca Nueva, 1975).
*Cita con la vida* (Madrid: Biblioteca Nueva, 1976).
*El tiempo es un río lentísimo de fuego* (Barcelona: Ediciones 29, 1978).
*La noche oscura del cuerpo* (Madrid: Biblioteca Nueva, 1980).
*Desde nunca* (Barcelona: Libros Río Nuevo, 1982).
*Derramen su sangre las sombras* (Madrid: Torremozas, 1983).
*Del obligado dolor* (Madrid: Almarabú, 1984).
*Cráter* (Madrid: Biblioteca Nueva, 1985).
*Hermosos días en China* (Madrid: Torremozas, 1983).

35

### Anthologies of poetry

Díez de Revenga, Francisco Javier, ed., *Carmen Conde: Antología poética* (Madrid: Biblioteca Nueva, 2006).

Granados, Juana, ed. & trans., *Carmen Conde: Poesie* (Milano: Istituto Editoriale Cisalpino, 1953).

Hiriart, Rosario, ed., *Antología Poética* (Madrid: Espasa-Calpe, 1985).

Miró, Emilio, ed., *Obra poética de Carmen Conde: (1929–1966)* (Madrid: Biblioteca Nueva, 1967; 2nd ed. 1979).

Miró, Emilio, ed., *Poesía completa* (Madrid: Castalia, 2007).

### Select prose

These works are relevant to the introduction.

*El Escorial: Una meditación más* (Madrid: Raíz, 1948).

*Mi libro de El Escorial (meditaciones)* (Valladolid: Colegio Mayor Universitario de Santa Cruz, 1949).

*Empezando la vida: Memorias de una infancia en Marruecos: (1914–1920)* (Tetuán: Al-Motamid, 1955).

*Poesía ante el tiempo y la inmortalidad* (Madrid: Real Academia Española, 1979).

*Por el camino, viendo sus orillas*, 3 vols (Barcelona: Plaza y Janés, 1986).

*Empezando la vida: Memorias de una infancia en Melilla (1914–1920)* (Melilla: UNED, 1991).

## Critical works on Carmen Conde

For a writer of her stature and longevity, there is comparatively little critical work on Carmen Conde and almost nothing on *Mientras los hombres mueren*. Her centenary in 2007 saw an upsurge of critical interest in her life and work, and to that are due a full-length biography, an exhibition with an accompanying catalogue containing essays and reminiscences on Conde and tributes to her by poets and academics. This brief bibliography contains work of general interest or of direct relevance to *Mientras los hombres mueren*.

### Books and collections of essays

Díez de Revenga, Francisco Javier, ed., *Carmen Conde: voluntad creadora* (Murcia: Sociedad Estatal de Conmemoraciones Culturales, 2007).

Díez de Revenga, Francisco Javier and de Paco, Mariano, eds, *En un pozo de lumbre*: *Estudios sobre Carmen Conde* (Murcia: Patronato Carmen Conde-Antonio Oliver/Fundación Cajamurcia, 2007).

Ferris, José Luis, *Carmen Conde: Vida, pasión y verso de una escritora olvidada* (Madrid: Temas de hoy, 2007).

de Luis, Leopoldo, *Carmen Conde* (Madrid: Ministerio de Cultura, 1982).

**Articles and chapters of books**

Díaz-Plaja, Guillermo, 'Discurso', in Conde, Carmen, *Poesía ante el tiempo y la inmortalidad*, pp. 55–76.

Evans, Jo, 'Carmen Conde's *Mujer sin Edén:* Controversial Notions of Sin', in Davies, Catherine, ed., *Women Writers in Spain and Twentieth-Century Latin America* (Lampeter: Edwin Mellen Press, 1993), pp. 71–83.

Fernández Hernández, Caridad, 'Cronología', in Diez de Revenga, Francisco Javier, ed., *Carmen Conde: Voluntad creadora*, pp. 57–66.

Miró, Emilio, 'La pasión o la vida', in Díez de Revenga, Francisco Javier, ed., *Carmen Conde: Voluntad creadora*, pp. 131–145.

Miró, Emilio, 'La poesía civil de Carmen Conde', in Díez de Revenga, Francisco Javier and de Paco, Mariano, eds., *En un pozo de lumbre: Estudios sobre Carmen Conde*, pp. 233–256.

de la Paz, Pilar Nieva, 'Una polémica politico-literaria en torno a la incorporación de la mujer a la Real Academia Española (1978): ¿Rosa Chacel o Carmen Conde?', *Voz y letra*, XV, 2, 2004, pp. 105–113.

Prieto de Paula, Ángel L., 'Carmen Conde, la primera mujer', *El País*, 11 August 2007

Quance, Roberta, 'Norah Borges Illustrates Two Spanish Women Poets', in Bonaddio, Federico and de Ros, Xon, eds, *Crossing Fields in Modern Spanish Culture* (Oxford: Legenda, 2003), pp. 54–66.


## Works on the Spanish Civil War

### Poetry

Alberti, Rafael, *Capital de la gloria*, in *Poesías completas* (Buenos Aires: Losada, 1961), pp. 401–423.

de Luis, Leopoldo, ed., *Miguel Hernández: Poemas sociales, de guerra y de muerte* (Madrid: Alianza, 1989).

Prados, Emilio, ed., *Romancero general de la guerra de España* (Valencia: Ediciones Españolas, 1937).

Sánchez Saornil, Lucía, *Romancero de mujeres libres*, in *Poesía*, ed., Martín Casamitjana, Rosa María (Valencia: Pre-Textos/IVAM, 1996), pp. 113–140.

de Vicente Hernando, César, ed., *Poesía de la guerra civil española 1936–39* (Madrid: Ediciones Akal, 1994).


### Books

Beevor, Antony, *The Battle for Spain: The Spanish Civil War, 1936–1939* (New York/London: Penguin, 2006).

Carr, Raymond, *The Civil War in Spain 1936–39* (London: Weidenfeld and Nicolson, 1986).

Preston, Paul, *The Spanish Civil War, 1936–39* (London: Weidenfeld and Nicolson, 1986).

Preston, Paul, *The Coming of the Spanish Civil War: Reform, Reaction and Revolution in the Second Republic* (London: Routledge, 1994).

Thomas, Hugh, *The Spanish Civil War* (London: Hamilton, 1977).

### Articles, films and websites including related issues

Armengou, Montse and Belis, Richard, *Los niños perdidos del franquismo* (Barcelona: Plaza y Janés, 2002).

Bowen, Wayne H., 'Pilar Primo de Rivera and the Axis Temptation', *The Historian*, I, 67 (Spring) 2005, pp. 62–72.

Cercas, Javier, *Soldados de Salamina* (Barcelona: Tusquets, 2001).

Cobb, Christopher, 'The Republican State and Mass Educational-Cultural Initiatives', *Spanish Cultural Studies*, pp. 133–138.

Cué, Carlos E. 'La ley de memoria se aprueba entre aplausos de invitados antifranquistas', *El País*, 10 November 2007.

Díaz, Elías, 'The Left and the Legacy of Francoism: Political Culture in Opposition and Transition', *Spanish Cultural Studies*, pp. 283–294.

Graham, Helen and Labanyi, Jo, eds, *Spanish Cultural Studies: An Introduction* (Oxford: Oxford University Press, 1995).

Graham, Helen, 'Gender and the State: Women in the 1940s', *Spanish Cultural Studies*, pp. 182–195.

Graham, Helen, 'Women and Social Change', *Spanish Cultural Studies*, pp. 99–115.

Haffner, Sebastian, 'Spain – The Legend and the Reality', *Observer*, 22 March 1959.

Lannon, Frances, *Privilege, Persecution and Prophecy: The Catholic Church in Spain 1875–1975* (Oxford: Clarendon Press, 1987).

Ministerio de Trabajo y Asuntos Sociales, 'Los niños de la guerra', DGE-SGONI, 11 May 2006, acc. www:ciudadaniaexterior.mtas.es.

Trueba, David, *Soldados de Salamina* (Warner, 2003).

## Books on women's writing/war memory in Spain 1900–39

Davies, Catherine, *Spanish Women's Writing, 1849–1996* (London: Athlone Press, 1998).

Mangini, Shirley, *Memories of Resistance: Women's Voices from the Spanish Civil War* (New Haven: Yale University Press, 1995).

Martínez, Josebe, *Exiliadas: escritoras, guerra civil y memoria* (Barcelona: Montesinos, 2007).

O'Neill, Carlota, *Una mujer en la guerra de España* (Madrid: Oberon, 2003).

Preston, Paul, *Doves of War: Four Women of the Spanish Civil War* (London: Harper Collins, 2002).

*Mientras los hombres mueren*

*Mientras los hombres mueren fue escrito en un tiempo de intenso dolor por lo que la guerra destruía y seguirá destruyendo. No unos hombres determinados, sino todos los hombres son llorados aquí con el profundo desconsuelo que siente una mujer ante los inescrutables designios que permiten el horror donde vivía la sonrisa confiada.*

*Los poemas «A los niños muertos en la guerra», que figuran en este mismo libro, me fueron arrancados de la entraña con más profunda desesperación todavía.*

*Todo dolor es inútil, lo supe entonces y lo sé mejor ahora. Y, sin embargo, decir en voz alta cuánto se está sufriendo por lo irremediable parece que borra todos los límites entre los demás y nosotros.*

*Y ese fue el único consuelo que entonces encontré.*

## Commentary

The title Conde uses in the handwritten or autograph manuscript is 'Poemas a los niños muertos en la guerra'. The sub-heading used for them in *Obra poética* (2nd ed., Madrid: Biblioteca Nueva, 1979) on which she collaborated closely with the editor, Emilio Miró (p. 207), 'A los niños muertos por la guerra', is perhaps even more poignant; the children did not simply die in the war, they died because of it. Miró maintains this use of alternate titles in his *Carmen Conde: Poesía completa* (Madrid: Castalia, 2007, pp. 161–178, p. 161).

This is the preface included in the first complete edition of *Mientras los hombres mueren*, published in Milan in 1953 (Milan: Istituto Editoriale Cisalpino, 1953) on the instigation of Conde's friend and champion, the Italian-based, Spanish academic, Juana Granados. In the intervening 14 years, the Franco dictatorship had become well entrenched in Spain and those who remained after the Nationalist victory had had to resign themselves to making their way as best they could despite the tremendous restrictions imposed on them. Meanwhile, much of the rest of Europe was

41

still in the difficult throes of recovery from the devastation of the Second World War which had only ended, in Europe, eight years previously. The conciliatory and humanitarian tone of this preface is therefore understandable as a response to the specifics of the situation in Spain and more generally in post-war Europe. However, it is less likely that her sympathies were always so impartial at the time of writing.

As Miró observes (*Poesía completa*, p. 41) during this time Conde invoked biblical references in an attempt to encompass the destruction she was witnessing: 'comprendí cuánto pesa el Eclesiastés; sobre todo en quien sólo había leído a Sulamita'. *Sulamita* is a reference to the Shulamite woman, possibly a young female attendant or lover of King Solomon's, mentioned once and briefly in the *Song of Solomon*, also known as the *Song of Songs* (Chapter 6, Verse 13): 'Return, return O Shulamite; return, return that we may look upon thee.' In some accounts this attendant is believed to have deserted Solomon to live with a lowly shepherd lover. The *Song of Solomon* is regarded as the most lyrical book in the Bible; on one level it is a deeply erotic love poem, while, on another, Christian mystics, San Juan de la Cruz in particular, have taken it as a basis for meditation on the intimate relationship between the soul and God. (See his *Cántico espiritual*.) The *Book of Ecclesiastes*, which precedes the *Song of Solomon* is of a very different tenor, being a warning to the faithful that 'vanity of vanities, [...] all is vanity' (12:8) and one which emphasises the burdens and hardship which humans must bear in a world in which nothing is what it seems. Conde's shock is therefore that of one moving from a metaphorical and real land of poetry and plenty to one of apocalyptic destruction.

In the following commentaries, I refer to 'Conde' when discussing the craft of the poet or autobiographical influence and 'the speaker' when tracing the imagery of the poems themselves.

# Poem I

Mientras los hombres mueren os digo yo, la que canta desoladas provincias del Duelo, que se me rompen sollozos y angustias contra barcos de ébano furibundo; y la fruta par de mis labios quema de suspiros porque los cielos se han dejado hincar imprecaciones sombrías.

A los hombres que mueren yo los sigo en su buscar por entre las raíces y los veneros fangosos, pues ellos y yo tenemos igual designio de ensueño debajo de la tierra.

¡Cállense todos los que no se sientan doblar de agonía hoy, día de espanto abrasado por teas de gritos, que esta mujer os dice que la muerte está en no ver, ni oír, ni saber, ni morir!

## Commentary

In Conde's autograph manuscript there is a dedication in square brackets [J.R.J.] at the bottom. J.R.J is Juan Ramón Jiménez.

**Paragraph 1:** The word *duelo* is used to represent pain, suffering, sorrow, even torment. It is capitalised here. The speaker evokes the *provincias del Duelo* in order to constitute a topography or geography of pain and loss. *El Duelo* is a river which runs through various provinces, all of them associated with suffering. There is an inevitable echo of the word *Duero* (*Douro* in Portuguese, Galician and English) in *Duelo*. The Douro/ Duero is one of the great rivers of the Iberian peninsula. It runs from the province of Soria in Castilla-León to Oporto on the Portuguese Atlantic coast. The *suspiros* (sighs) and *angustias* (anguish, suffering, anxiety), her sighs and suffering, break against the *barcos de ébano furibundo* like great waves on this river Duelo. The darkness (ebony) and the furious nature (*furibundo*) of the colour used to describe the boats on the river add to the atmosphere of storm and foreboding. *La fruta par* of her lips, the paired fruit (each of the lips being a fruit, both lips constituting a pair) is burning with sighs (*quema de suspiros*). The image of lips burning with sighs would traditionally be part of a love poem, where the lover's sighs are an indication of (as yet) unrequited or unsatisfied love. Here, it indicates a very different universe. *Hincar imprecaciones sombrías* communicates violence done to the skies. In this act of violence, the passive skies have allowed themselves to be outraged. This is conveyed in *se han dejado*, they have permitted this to happen to them. The outrage described in the verb *hincar* is the action of thrusting a sharp object, like a stake or a spear, into something soft, such as earth or the body of a living being. Instead of sharp objects, *imprecaciones* (curses, that is when a person or object is cursed by someone so that evil will befall them) are thrust into the skies, which have done nothing to resist. Conde uses the adjective *sombrías*, meaning dark or sombre, to add to the sense of evil and impending doom. As this is the opening poem, it may be a general evocation of the awful fate which has overtaken Spain with the outbreak of war, or it might anticipate the concentration, later in the collection, on the manner in which death, in the form of bombs, rained down on the population from the skies and the sea.

**Paragraph 2:** The fallen soldiers' bodies will remain on the land. Buried or not those bodies will gradually decay into the earth. She imagines the soldiers searching through the mud and the roots beneath the surface of the earth, looking for their fate. *Designio* can mean a plan or design, *ensueño* a dream or a fantasy, in the sense of a dream come true. *Designio de ensueño* might then be a future which is fantasised about or planned for. However, in this case, there is no connotation of a fairytale come true. Its place has been taken by the opposite, a dystopia of previously unimaginable proportions.

**Paragraph 3:** The use of *teas* (hand-held, flaming torches) to describe the cries of those suffering recalls the torchlight used in political pageantry in the 1930s, so beloved of fascists of all nations. The *teas de gritos* might refer, on one level, to the suffering of the afflicted and, on another, to the roars of support and enthusiasm of fascist crowds. The *teas* might thus be a reference to the bombing raids in which the *día de espanto*, this day of horror, is burning (*abrasado*). The message *esta mujer*, the voice of these poems, has to impart: that death lies in not seeing, hearing, knowing or dying, appears, for the first three verbs, to be a statement of the plainly obvious. However, in the fourth, *morir*, she produces a paradox, to the effect that death lies in not dying which forces a re-evaluation of the statement. One possibility is that those who refuse to become involved in the war, those who do their best to ignore it by not being disposed to see or hear, by not being willing to know, and do not put their lives on the line are the ones who truly suffer death.

pacifist - who opposes
violence + war
- this criticizes what
would be a
pacifist?

# Poem II

¿Ninguna mano puede sacar el puñal que me ha multiplicado en el corazón?... ¿Son los felices de pan, o los heridos de pánico, los míos? Llevo mis dedos al costado que fue de Cristo y me zumba la sangre de dos mil años de terror inútil.

¿Quién monta esos caballos azules fríos que corren las mesetas donde el pasado alzó murallas de Ávila y Segovia trágicas? ¿Qué cinturas metálicas de guerreros se bañan en el Tajo y en el Guadalquivir, por donde se tradujo al romance Atenas y Arabia?

La tierra está nutrida de simientes frescas, porque los seres que se le incorporan, desfrutecidos, devuelven intacto el caudal de generaciones que no tuvieron tiempo de crear.

¡Y mi corazón en puñal, como el vuestro, hermanos de la sangre en llamas, tiene cada día más rotas sus geografías de latidos!

**Commentary**

**Paragraph 1:** The dagger (*puñal*) multiplying in her heart may be a reference to Our Lady of Sorrows, *La virgen de los dolores*. The Blessed Virgin is sometimes represented in this avocation (where emphasis is placed on a specific quality associated with the Blessed Virgin) with her heart pierced by seven swords to denote the seven sorrows of her life. The identification of the speaker with the Blessed Virgin, mother of humanity, is not, however, total, since the Virgin saw her son sacrificed to save humanity whereas, in contrast, the speaker in these poems has no children of her own and actively refuses to have any while the war continues.

Food was scarce in the Republican zone between 1937 and 1939 as Republican supply lines were increasingly disrupted by Nationalist forces. *Los felices de pan* are those who are lucky enough to have bread to eat; they contrast with those, *los heridos de pánico*, wounded by panic. The reference to *pan* here may also be related to the sacrifice of Christ on the Cross, celebrated in the conversion of bread into the body of Christ in the Sacrament of the Eucharist. This association is continued in the next sentence.

Christ's body traditionally has five wounds from the crucifixion, one in each hand where it was pierced by a nail, one in each foot and one in his side where a Roman centurion pierced him with his lance because Christ, hanging on the cross, was not yet dead (John 19:34). *Llevo mis dedos al costado* refers to Christ's meeting, after his Resurrection, with his disciple, Thomas, who refused to believe he was the Risen Christ, until Christ allowed him to put his fingers into the wound in his side. Ever since, this episode has been cited when someone refuses to believe something they are told unless there is palpable evidence for it. *Dos mil años de terror inútil* refers to the almost two thousand years which have elapsed since the birth of Christ, and to all the war and suffering, the useless (*inútil*) war and suffering, much of it linked to religion, which the Christain world and its neighbours have seen, in spite of the message of peace and mutual understanding that Christ preached in the Gospel. *Me zumba la sangre*, the speaker feels all this blood beating in her or around her (*zumbar*, to hum). This is cumulatively all the blood spilt from the time of Christ to the present day, the blood actually coursing through her own body, and the blood of those suffering and dying in the Civil War.

**Paragraph 2:** *Las mesetas* are the high, arid plains of Castilla-León. The reference is to to the tales in the Spanish ballad tradition, the *romancero*, of the medieval Christian knights who galloped along these plains and took part in chivalrous battles with Moorish knights. In the traditional ballads the respect of Christian and Moorish knights for each other is mutual and unquestioned, as is their observance of a strict code of honour in battle. Now the horses are *azules*, *fríos*, and riderless. The blue may be the blue of the sky, the cold may be that of the high plateau, the inference that these are ghostly presences, a hearkening back to an age of chivalry which bears no resemblance to present carnage. Ávila and Segovia are the two cities in Castilla-León with the most completely preserved Moorish and medieval architectural heritage. The historic centres of these cities would have been there at the time of these fabled chivalrous knights and the real-life soldiers of fortune, conscripted peasants and Christian barons and Muslim lords who fought skirmishes against each other in the Middle Ages. When both cities were occupied by Nationalist forces in July 1936, the troops encountered little local resistance and thus these two iconic medieval cities remained largely intact. Much of the propagandistic poetry published in newspapers and magazines, on both sides, during the Civil War was in ballad (*romance*) form. These modern *romances* habitually hearkened back to the heroes, real and mythical, of the Reconquest and lauded the generals of the Republican or National-ist armies in similar terms as heroes of a great battle against a dastardly enemy. As distinct from the *romance* tradition, no compliments were paid to the enemy, no courteous quarter given or expected. It has to be said that this style was more prevalent on the Nationalist side, where the campaign was also presented as a crusade (*cruzada*) to restore Spain to the Catholic Church. The use of *trágicas* to describe the walls of Ávila and Segovia may thus be seen as a reflection of the contrast between the idealised past of the *romances* and the sordid present, convulsed in a frenzy of fraternal blood-letting.

The *cinturas metálicas* allude to the coats of armour worn by knights; literally it indicates their waists, which may be understood as torsos, coated in chainmail or plate armour. It is worth remembering that the *cintura* is also frequently cited as a, usually female, erotic zone in lyric poetry. The Tagus (*Tajo*) and Guadalquivir are two of the great rivers of the Iberian peninsula. The Tagus rises in the Albarraicín mountains in the Province of Teruel in Aragon and flows into the sea at Lisbon. The Guadalquivir begins in the Cazorla mountains in Jaén province in Andalusia, flows through Cordoba and Seville and debouches into the Gulf of Cadiz near Sanlúcar de Barrameda. *Se tradujo al romance Atenas y Arabia* evokes the importance of literary and scientific culture in the Kingdom of Al-Andalus during the 700 years, from 710 to 1492, of its existence. Much of the culture of Al-Andalus, achievements in mathemat-ics, astronomy, agriculture, philospohy and literature gradually filtered into Christian consciousness and into *romance*, the indigenous language of the Iberian peninsula, one dialect of which eventually developed into Castilian. Learned culture in Al-Andalus also retained a significant part of the knowledge of Ancient Greek and, to a lesser extent, Roman civili-sation and access to sources, primarily in the great library of Alexandria, in Egypt, with which the rest of Western Europe temporarily lost touch after the final decline of the Roman Empire in the late fifth century. The word *romance* may also, of course, allude to the Spanish traditional ballad which was not merely restricted to the doings of chivalrous knights on the borders of Al-Andalus. The actions, loves and sorrows of heroes and heroines from Greek and Roman mythology and Arab legend were recounted with similar gusto. In the Civil War reality, however, the suggestion is that any such warriors or *cinturas metálicas* are floating dead in these great rivers.

**Paragraph 3:** *Los simientes* are the seeds, the fresh seeds contained in the bodies of all the young people who are being killed and whose bodies are now rotting into the ground. These seeds have not been used, so the bodies are *desfrutecidos*, deprived of the fruit they might have borne (i.e. the children they did not have time to engender) and all the genetic inheritance of generations, *el caudal de generaciones*, is returned unused to the soil.

**Paragraph 4:** The speaker's heart is now in the shape of a single dagger (*en puñal*). Her heart has an internal geography of beats (*sus geografías de latidos*), as if she has internalised the national topography of rivers, plains and cities now torn apart by the actions of war. She speaks to her brothers *de la sangre en llamas*. These flames are as much to do with the destruction brought about by battle and bombing raids as with the passions aroused in the blood of those going into battle.

# Poem III

En la más ahondada raíz del mar clavaron mis hermanos sus gritos de terror: ¡No queremos morir!—y los ojos hacían más azules a los gritos. Y el mar se fue creciendo, monte y monte denso de carne verde con cuellos de alados encajes, hasta que el cielo lo recibió poseyéndolo en clamores.

Yo iba por las noches negras, sin rosas de sol en mi frente. ¿Cómo encender mis sienes si aquellos a los que yo amaba tanto apagaban sus brasas en el gemido desbocado del morir?

¡Dadme un barco con el más esbelto pabellón de sonrisas para alcanzar el llanto que brotas tú, Mar, y que nacen los míos en agonía desbordante! ¡Que yo quiero ser fuerte, que yo quiero ser ágil, que yo contendré la vida que se derrama por la vid de los muertos!

## Commentary

**Paragraph 1:** The field of battle has moved, briefly, to the sea. The use of *clavar* (to nail) echoes the use of the verb *hincar* to describe the violence emanating from the skies, in Poem I (*los cielos se han dejado imprecaciones sombrías*). Here, the driving action is performed by *mis hermanos*, the men dying in battle, probably at sea in this instance. Thus, they plunge their cries into the deepest root of the sea (*la más ahondada raíz del mar*). The use of the verb *clavar* carries a connotation of the nails driven into the flesh of Christ on the Cross, alluded to in Poem II. The adjective *azules*, as in Poem II (*esos caballos azules fríos*), continues the association which seems to imply death, with the blue here being, to some extent, also the blue of the sea.

However, this is an angry green sea. The *alados encajes*, collars of lace or lace which looks as if it has wings (*alas*) might be foam on the seawater as it rises, but this is a sea full of bodies. Their flesh is green (*carne verde*), either because the sea itself is green and stormy or because the bodies are decomposing, or indeed both. At the same time, wings might be associated with angels, and with the upward movement which carries the sea ever higher until it meets the sky. The heavens then take in the bodies amid great clamour.

**Paragraph 2:** The speaker has no *rosas de sol*, no colour in her face (*frente* is forehead but here the general meaning is face); the sense is that she has not been out in daylight for some time. She is also subject to insomnia (*yo iba por las noches negras*) and is thus a creature of the night, when terrors are at their greatest.

The worst of these is *el gemido desbocado del morir*. The trembling of death (*gemir* is to tremble) as experienced by her brothers at war is *desbocado*, out of control, in the sense of overpowering, uncontainable, like a horse which has bolted (*desbocar*). To reiterate the statement about having no colour in her cheeks, she moves on to her temples (*sienes*, the part of the head in front of and above the ears), usually associated with wisdom and thought, and, in a rhetorical question, (*¿cómo encender mis sienes?*) explains that she can no more be fired up intellectually than she can have the sunlight on her brow, not while her brothers are dying. The allusion to fire present in *encender* is then echoed in the use of *brasas*, the embers of those whom she loved, now engulfed by death.

**Paragraph 3:** There is bitter contrast here between the boat with the sleekest pavilion of smiles (*el más esbelto pabellón de sonrisas*) which she asks for (*dadme un barco*) in order that she may set forth to reach the lament which the sea causes to rise out of itself (*que brotas tú*) and which is born of her brothers (*y que nacen los míos*) in the overwhelming agony (*en agonía desbordante*) of death and fear of death.

In this boat, she aims to contain (*yo contendré*) all the life which is now being spilled (*la vida que se derrama*) even as it spreads along the vine (*la vid*) to which the dead, like grapes, are attached. Somehow, she will be the saviour.

no pacifista

# Poem IV

¡El duelo!
Vienen gritando las voces por entre las alamedas de suspiros.
¡El duelo!
Vienen gritando las madres sobre ascuas desorbitadas de llantos.
　¡El duelo! ¡El duelo! ¡El duelo!—grito yo, sola, río de orillas quemadas.
Y hay luces sin llamas, pánicos en clavos largos a la carne sacudida, bajo mi
duelo conciencia del espíritu.

## Commentary

**Paragraphs (Lines) 1–4:** *Ascuas* are embers. *Estar sobre ascuas* is to be in
a state of painful suspense or tension. *Vienen gritando sobre ascuas* offers
the image of the mothers walking along a path of embers, walking on hot
coals effectively. The adjective *desorbitada* is employed when, for example,
someone is startled and their eyes pop out of their head, or literally they
are almost knocked out of their sockets. This might indicate the startled,
stressed condition of the mothers though it applies more directly to the
embers. These embers are themselves formed of *llantos*. Thus *ascuas desorbitadas de llantos* carries the sense of suspense, pain, shock and sorrow, and
the complete image is of mothers who come crying out (*¡el duelo!*) along
an *alameda* (avenue) *de suspiros*, as if the grieving sighs (*suspiros*) were
trees lining the road.

　The speaker shouts out, as she sees the mothers coming, as if she were
a river with its banks burned (*río de orillas quemadas*). There is a progres-
sion from the *alameda*, down which the *voces* come in a group, to the river
which she feels herself to embody and where she is alone. *El duelo* flows
along this river too. Her cry (*¡El duelo! ¡el duelo! ¡el duelo!*) answers and
echoes the mothers.

　The procession of mothers appears to merge with the river, its banks
burned, at this point. There are lights without flames (*luces sin llamas*),
fits of panic in the form of or which feel like long nails (*pánicos en clavos*

*largos*) inserted into the (already) shaken or shocked flesh (*a la carne sacudida*). All this takes place beneath the speaker's pain (*mi duelo*) which is, in its essence, a spiritual awareness (*conciencia del espíritu*). The mention of *clavos* carries, yet again, a reference to the passion of Christ with the variation that the flesh pierced here is female, that of the mothers, that of the speaker. The *luces sin llamas* which process down the road hearken back to the *teas de gritos* of Poem I, part of a desperate and ironic continuum which melds pain and pageantry.

Mater
dolorosa

# Poem V
## La muerte en el aire

Alguien contó en la desguarnecida noche, sin ángeles, una desgarradora música de lágrimas. Los seres que ya se liberaron del espanto del día estridencial de duelos escucharon con voraz oreja y aprendieron los golpes estrictos del corazón arrastrando de la almohada.

Quien decía, habló de continentes y de volcadas mares; pero una primavera sencilla de hojas, sin riesgos de plumas, hizo el contrapunto agudo. Los que atendían, sonrieron dichosos de oler el azul de la vida tierna.

¡Ay de los desvelados que ninguna promesa, ninguna palabra duermen en dicha!

Se quedarán fijos, eternos abiertos ojos despavoridos contra los abismos en donde la voz de la muerte rueda piedra sin musgo, serpea río con espinas.


**Commentary**

*En el aire* might refer to planes in the sky or, in a more general sense, to what is 'in the air'; *un aire* may also be a tune or air.

**Paragraph 1:** *La desguarnecida noche* is an ungarrisoned night, a night with no soldiers on guard. This is a night which is *sin ángeles*. Perhaps this indicates that the garrison troops are not soldiers but guardian angels. In Catholic tradition, each person is accompanied through life by a guardian angel. Here, the guardian angels are not present, rendering the night even more dangerous. In this night, there is someone, unidentified, singing or telling about or following the beat of (*contar*) a mournful music. *Desgarradora*, which means tearing or ripping, might describe the effect that listening to such *música de lágrimas* might have on the listener. This music contrasts sharply with the music usually associated with angels: celestial music of harps and singing, rejoicing and secure in the presence of God.

*Los golpes estrictos del corazón* might denote the heartbeat of the listeners but also the beat of this music. These listeners are *arrastrando de la almohada*, perhaps because they are in bed, unable to sleep, dragging the pillow around after them, tossing and turning. Yet they listen with an eager ear (*con voraz oreja*). *Ya se liberaron del espanto del día estridencial de duelos* might imply that they are, in fact, either dreaming or in a half-conscious state, freed from the awfulness of the day, but not at rest. *Estridencial* comes from *estridente*, strident; it has been a day of strident horror and suffering. Since *estridencial* might be said to convey a particularly steely and harsh quality of sound, this may be what is reflected in the *desgarradora música de lágrimas*.

**Paragraph 2:** *Contrapunto*, counterpoint is a musical term used to describe a piece of music in which there are, in effect, two melodies, played simultaneously, each acting as a balance and a contrast to the other. Here, the song (*quien decía* refers to *alguien contó*) of continents and seas which have been emptied out (*volcadas*) finds its counterpoint in a simple spring of leaves, in which there was no risk of feathers (*sin riesgo de plumas*). This may be an idealised past, or simply peacetime. The *riesgo de plumas* also, on another level, takes the imagery back to an awareness that the night is ungarrisoned, *sin ángeles*, and at the same time seems to suggest that this is a good thing, since the presence of feathers, even those on angels' wings, is somehow an indicator of menace. In a very practical sense, that risk is bombers with deadly payloads in the sky, as indicated in the title.

*Oler el azul de la vida tierna* suggests that tender life might bring the focus to innocence and hope. Here, the colour blue reinforces this, because of its associations with the ethereal and with blue skies. This is in contrast to the use of *azul* in Poems II and III which appears to be negative. The deliberate confusion of the senses (synaesthesia) in the idea of smelling a colour shows Conde's debt to the aesthetics of symbolist decadence with its emphasis on heightened sensual perception.

**Paragraph 3:** *Los desvelados* are those unable to sleep, to whom no promise, no word will bring sleep. They contrast with those who are able to sleep, after a fashion, while listening to the *desgarradora música de lágrimas*. In this the speaker refers to herself, she cannot sleep.

**Paragraph 4:** Those who cannot sleep are fixated on the abysses where death stalks, their eternally watching eyes *despavoridos*, horror-struck. The voice of death is a rolling stone, which, by definition, gathers no moss, *piedra sin musgos.* It is also a *río con espinas*, a river with thorns in it, or, since another possible meaning of *espina* is fishbone, a river with fishbones in it, possibly because the fish are also dead. In another sense, the eyes of those who cannot sleep are eternally open, perhaps the *río con espinas* is a reference to the sore eyes insomniacs often suffer from. This soreness might be described as a sensation of having thorns in one's eyes.

# Poem VI

La tierra quebrada, resollada, resquebrajante, hecha púa de corazones secos, vasija de sexos adolescentes sin abrir. La tierra florida de sangres, de ojos deshechos, de senos escurridos. La tierra agujereada de gritos, de espumas, con rodillas de sollozos y de estertores.

¡La gran tierra de mi padre hecho tierra!

Recorriéndola grano a grano, descalzados, sedientos, pegando los labios al corro de arena transformada que es el agua, oiremos a los muertos, a los asesinados, a los suicidas, a los estallados con dinamita. En la oscuridad agria, punzadora, de la tierra solamente ya Tierra.

## Commentary

**Paragraph 1:** *La tierra quebrada, resollada, resquebrajante* means respectively: shattered or broken, out of breath or with baited breath, cracked. This land has become a *púa de corazones secos*. *Una púa* is a spine or a needle, the earth has become one big spine or needle made of dried hearts. It is a *vasija de sexos adolescentes*, a vessel for adolescent genitalia, *sin abrir*, which have not opened, that is ripened or come to fruition, which have not produced young.

The adjective *florida* would normally be used to indicate the flowers growing on the land. This land, however, has *sangres, ojos desechos, senos escurridos*, instead. This is the blood of all the individual dead mixed together, their eyes torn out of their sockets, the flat chests of the young (soldiers and children), possibly also the flaccid breasts of the old.

The land is full of the holes made by those crying out (*agujereada de gritos*) and the holes made by foam (*espumas*), perhaps the foam on the mouths of the wounded and dying. There are also knees bent with sobbing (*rodillas de sollozos*), grieving at their own deaths or the deaths of others, and with death rattles (*estertores*), the sound made by a person's breathing at the point of death.

**Paragraph 2:** There is a play on both meanings of *tierra* here, *tierra* or land as earth in which crops are grown and bodies are buried; and *tierra* as nation. *La gran tierra de mi padre* might be an allusion to Spain as a great nation, venerated by her father's generation and a despairing reflection on what it has become, a battlefield piled up with the war dead. A fatherland (*patria*) has become nothing more than earth in which the dead decompose. Up to and including this line, no verbs are used. The poem offers an unrelenting list of the terrible qualities of the land in time of war.

**Paragraph 3:** The speaker now moves to the plural, and she speaks for a group which is shoeless (*descalzado*) and thirsty, attempting to find water and finding their lips stuck to *el corro de arena transformada*, a pit or patch of sand which, transformed, is what the water is now made from in this place. As they run over the land grain of earth by grain (*grano a grano*) what they will hear is the noise of the dead, the murdered, those who have committed suicide and those who have been blown up by dynamite.

All of this takes place in a land which is covered by darkness. This darkness is bitter (*agria*) and characterised by its biting quality. The adjective *punzadora*, from *punzar*, to punch a hole in something or to puncture, turns it into a darkness which causes sharp, stabbing pain. The capitalisation of *Tierra* at the end builds on the meanings of *tierra* established earlier. This is *Tierra* as the planet Earth, it brings with it a sense of cosmic isolation, and removes the conflict from the context of a familiar homeland to the much more impersonal one of the planet itself.

# Poem VII

Yacedoras y yacedores, enderezaos siquiera mientras los corceles de ébano del duelo golpean con sus crines ese aire de España.

Abandonad vuestros lechos frenéticos de lujuria, hembras y varones que jamás seréis mujeres ni hombres. Arrostrad por un tiempo el vaivén de vuestras horizontales cabezas; que la corteza de sangre en donde iréis a pudriros sepa que podéis caminar sin remar noches de espasmo.

Mundo aún tendido, álzate. Que el dolor purifica hasta a aquellos que no lo merecen.

## Commentary

**Paragraph 1:** The verb *yacer* is employed to describe the dead lying on their deathbeds or in their coffins. Male and female dead are distinguished here: *yacedores y yacedoras*. The use of *yacedoras* draws specific attention to the female dead, who might otherwise have been understood to form part of the plural *yacedores*. There is an echo here of the distinction made between addressing a mixed gender group as *señores* and as *señores y señoras*. The second is viewed as more polite, at the very least a courtesy extended to women on social occasions. These dead are instructed by the speaker to *enderezaos*, to stand or straighten up, to pay attention. *Siquiera* indicates that they must do this while *los corceles*, the galloping steeds, as in the mounts of medieval, chivalric knights, are beating with their manes (*sus crines*) against the *aire de España*. These steeds are black as ebony and they represent *el duelo*. These horses are the negation of the trusty steeds of medieval knights. Black is the traditional colour of mourning and they have taken on the function of mourners, almost always female in the Spanish context, who lead the community in its grief. *Este aire de España* might be seen here as the air in the sense of the air one breathes but also the state of war in which Spain finds itself.

**Paragraph 2:** The speaker calls on these dead to abandon their *lechos fréneticos de lujuria*. *Un lecho*, literally a bed, here is more likely to be a deathbed or a slab of marble or stone on which a dead body is laid out. Here she characterises the *lechos* as frenetic (*fréneticos*) and lustful (*de lujuria*), an evident and sarcastic contradiction since they are dead; they did not choose to die and furthermore they were young people who did not reach adulthood before they died and cannot do so now they are dead.

*Arrostrar* is to confront; the speaker is asking the dead to face up to the vertigo (*el vaivén*) they might experience if they were to lift their heads after so much time lying flat (*horizontales*). *La corteza*, here a place of blood in which they will rot (*iréis a pudriros*), may be construed as the bark of a tree or the cortex of the brain or the rind of a citrus fruit or the crust of the earth. However, *remar* is to row as in rowing a boat, and they must demonstrate to this *corteza* that they can walk without rowing along nights of spasm (*noches de espasmo*). The place where they will eventually rot might be seen as the land itself. It will be fertilised by their bodies but somehow before they succumb to this inevitability they must resist the vertigo induced by having lain horizontal for so long, resist the tendency to go into spasm or to have a fit, during the long night and stand, rising almost to attention, to honour the passing *duelo*.

**Paragraph 3:** The speaker repeats her exhortation here: *mundo aún tendido, álzate*. She claims that this is worth doing because pain, honouring pain as it passes by, will purify even those (of the dead) who are undeserving.

# Poem VIII

¿Qué cabeza trastornada sueña y sueña con la misma música que la mía?... ¡Me ha roto su soñar los puentes de ramas finas por donde mi sueño atravesaba bosques y ríos de lumbre!

¿Qué labios solitarios se besan a ellos mismos?

¿Qué voz se dice ternuras, se recuerda o se inventa diálogos imposibles?

¿Qué luz hay donde yo busco luz?

¡Dadme los sueños de las tácitas armonías, eterno reposo sin presentires en esta presente dramática conciencia de mi vida!

## Commentary

**Paragraph 1:** *Trastornada* can mean disturbed or traumatised. The speaker seeks another like herself, with the same music in his or her head. The question may be rhetorical in nature, implying that no being other than the speaker can dream about this music.

*Los puentes de ramas finas*, bridges made out of fine tree branches, appear to have interrupted the dreaming of this music, *su soñar*. *Me ha roto* is in the singular, but the sense is of *los puentes* acting in such unison they may be considered a single entity. *Bosques y ríos de lumbre*, woods and rivers of light provide the nocturnal or dream landscape along which her dreaming flowed.

**Paragraphs (lines) 2–4:** The first two lines record solitary, reflexive activities, lips kissing themselves, a voice engaged in dialogue with itself, uttering endearments to itself. The third line asks for a light which appears to be absent. The whole communicates the isolated, solitary condition of the speaker, the absence of light intensifies the lack of hope or indeed a visible community to which to belong.

**Paragraph 5:** The speaker wishes for dreams of *tácitas armonías*, harmonies which are not heard but which are understood. She looks for *un eterno reposo sin presentires*, an eternal repose without premonitions, a life in which there is no dread, no worry, no upheaval. Her present, of which she cannot escape continual awareness, is, of course, the inverse of what she dreams of and desires, *presente drámatica conciencia de mi vida*.

# Poem IX

Cierto que yo no pariré hijo de carne mientras la Tierra haya las furias amarillas de la Guerra.

Tú no estrenarás tu vientre mientras no tengan quietas sus fragancias todos los suelos por donde va el amor.

Yo me mantendré, sombrío luto, entre los muertos que fueron hijos de mujeres que nada pudieron contra su muerte.

## Commentary

**Paragraph (line) 1:** *Haya* (*haber*) is used in the sense of possession, meaning while on Earth the yellow furies of war (*las furias amarillas de la Guerra*) are still present, still an affliction; this will prevent her giving birth to a child. In classical mythology the Furies were the daughters of Gaia (Earth) and were conceived from the drops of blood which fell from Uranus (Heaven) when his son, Cronos, castrated him. They were thus born of family strife and their primary mission was to punish the perpetrators of murder within families. Since civil war is internecine conflict, the allusion to the Furies is that bit more telling in this context. Yellow, while often the colour of cowardice, also signifies hatred. Note that *Tierra* and *Guerra* are both personified here, deities at war. The speaker is vehement in her assertion that she will not have a child while War stalks the Earth.

**Paragraph (line) 2:** The use of *tú* here indicates either that she is addressing another woman, one representing all women caught up in this war, or she is addressing herself, in the reflexive way she employed in Poem VIII. The fragrances (*fragancias*) which are produced by *los suelos por donde va el amor* might once have been *quietas*, peaceful, idyllic even. Now, however, they are unquiet and these *suelos* are most likely battlefields, where love meets only death and destruction. It might even be that the *fragancias* now consist of the stench of death.

**Paragraph (line) 3:** Her resolution is to remain, in mourning or as the essence herself of solemn mourning, *sombrío luto*. She sees her role as that of keeping company with the dead (*los muertos que fueron hijos de mujeres*) whose own mothers could do nothing to prevent their dying.

- Maternidonga
- Sacrifici
- luto

# Poem X

Cada día tengo un hermano menos sobre la tierra, que se suma a los que dentro de las raíces yacen con las frentes vaciadas de ojos. Cada noche me duele más el sueño, porque si me enlaza, ¿cómo puedo gozarlo mientras los hombres mueren a marejadas? Y yo no duermo, ¡qué locura de noches con el horror presente de la guerra!

Me estoy quedando como un árbol al que le cortan todas sus ramas y sus hojas: ¡mi planta en el suelo, mis sienes en el aire, pero sin brazos para nadie! Si con brazos, ¿para quién, si todos mueren?

## Commentary

**Paragraph 1:** She returns to the image of the dead bodies intertwined with tree roots of Poem I. Here their eye sockets are empty, literally their foreheads (*frentes*) have been emptied (*vaciadas*) of eyes. Since the eyes are one of the first parts of the body, exposed soft tissue, to decompose or to be eaten by worms, predators or parasites, this observation is forensically accurate. Metaphorically, the eyeless foreheads of the dead suggests the powerlessness, isolation, disorientation of the dead as they lie in the soil.

The title of the collection appears in this next line, *mientras los hombres mueren*. The speaker uses sea imagery to convey the magnitude of the number of deaths; the men die in great ocean waves (*marejadas*). She cannot sleep, she cannot possibly let sleep wrap itself around her (*si me enlaza*) or let herself take pleasure in it (*gozarlo*) because she cannot sleep while the men are dying. She is awake every night, with only the horror of war for company, and it seems to her to be a form of madness (*locura de noches*). Since prolonged sleep deprivation does induce transitory mental illness, again the observation is both forensically correct and metaphorically powerful.

**Paragraph 2:** Here the speaker likens herself to a tree with neither branches or leaves, a negation of what a tree essentially is. She sees herself

65

with the soles of her feet (*mi planta*) in the ground, her temples (*sienes*) in the air, but she has no arms.

The rhetorical question (*¿para quién, si todos mueren?*) points to the redundancy of having arms if there is no-one left alive she can embrace. Since in Poem IX she has just made it clear that she will not have children in this time of war, it might be worth remembering that arms are used also to cradle children and that a tree without branches and leaves is incapable of regenerating itself, or even of remaining alive.

*mater dolorosa*

# Poem XI

¡Madres!... ¿O son las mares las que gritan con voz de parto para que se detenga la muerte en su siembra de yelos?

¡Madres!... ¿O son los olivos quienes retuercen sus conciencias de ramas ardorosas en ansiedad de lumbre sin fin?

¡Madres!... ¿O es que los que agonizan tienen un coro de estertores cuajando agrios verdes de espanto?

**Commentary**

There is a dedication in brackets (J.R.J.) at the bottom of the page in Conde's autograph manuscript.

**Paragraph (line) 1:** *Las mares* here is *los mares* in the manuscript. Generally, *la mar* is used in language which is more literary and where the essentially feminine nature of water as an element is relevant. In Conde's native Cartagena (Murcia), the popular pronunciation of *madres* and *mares* would be near indistinguishable, a factor which may be taken as reinforcing the essential femininity of the *las mares* here. The use of the feminine for the sea would be natural to all *cartageneros*, of course, because of the famous, salty lagoon, the *Mar Menor*, which lies north of Cartagena. Indeed, Conde went as far as dedicating a book of poetry to it, *Los poemas de Mar Menor* (Murcia: Universidad: 1962). The seas (mothers) are crying out, with the cry of a woman giving birth (*voz de parto*) in order to stop death in its path. Death is sowing (*la siembra* is the act of sowing) *yelos*. *Yelo* is a non-standard, archaic spelling for *hielo*. In agriculture, *yelos* (plural) is traditionally used to describe the severe frosts which can damage crops. Here it may also refer to the temperature of dead bodies.

**Paragraph (line) 2:** Just as the sea is an integral part of the Levantine landscape, so are olive groves. Here the olive trees are twisting (*retuercen*) their awareness of their own branches (*conciencias de ramas*). The branches or their consciousness of them is on fire (*ardorosas*). They are preoccupied or taken over by a longing for (*en ansiedad de*) an endless light (*lumbre sin fin*).

**Paragraph (line) 3:** Here it is as if all those who are dying (*los que agonizan*) are sounding the death rattle (*estertor*) in unison, as if they were a choir (*un coro de estertores*). This choir is setting or causing to coagulate (*cuajando*) the green citrus fruit (*agrios verdes*) of horror. This fruit is green because dead and dying are themselves immature.

Thus, the question in this poem might be: is it the mothers who are making this woeful noise or one of three alternatives: the seas, the olive groves, the dying? The sea, feminine grammatically and metaphorically, the olive trees, phallic, perhaps, and grammatically masculine, together encompass a totality, which can do nothing to pre-empt the slaughter and the death rattles.

# Poem XII

Yo sé bien que ninguna oreja egoísta se adapta a la esférica lumbre estallada de la tierra; por eso no suenan los pechos en voces ateridas, crecientes de horror, rechazando la muerte plural que llueve la negra lluvia sin fermento de trigo y sin fermento de limo.

¿Por qué no escucháis todos lo que yo escucho? Desgarro la noche con los ojos que mañana serán flores, para coger el resplandor sostenido de todos los ojos que cual los míos viven en la oscuridad doliente. Mi circulación recorre las mismas raíces que los zumos que socavan la tierra de tumbas, ¡y vivo con sangre de cirios en los labios, cirios que el pasado olvidó en imposibles altares de nubes a dioses de trágico sino, por estos hombres y por estos niños que se rajan en arteriales zumbidos bajo los edificios siniestros del llanto!

Yo sé bien cuán solos estamos los muertos y yo. Aunque mi frente sea de sol maduro y mis cabellos suban en raíces al cielo, ¡nadie dude jamás de esta angustia en que mueren mi cuerpo y mi alma!

## Commentary

**Paragraph 1:** The opening phrase melds the senses of hearing and vision. The selfish ear (*oreja egoísta*) cannot adapt to the light emanating from an explosion (*la esférica lumbre estallada de la tierra*). The use of *esférica* alludes to the round light of an explosion; it may also be said to invoke the spherical mass of molten rock at the Earth's core. The ear which cannot adapt to the sound of the exploding bomb or shell is perhaps described as selfish (*egoísta*) simply because of the natural human urge to survive, to avoid conflict. The use of *egoísta* may also be accusatory, in the sense that, if a (selfish) majority did not turn away from the consequences of war, then there might be an outcry of horror of sufficient magnitude to stop it. Thus, there are none in whose breasts their (own) horrified voices ring out in growing horror (*no suenan los pechos en voces ateridas, crecientes de horror*). There are no voices which reject, in unison, *la muerte plural*, this

69

death from multiple sources (*plural*) which pours down a black rain (*que llueve negra lluvia*) which does not increase the fertility (*sin fermento*) of either wheat (*trigo*) or mud (*limo*) and is therefore contrary to nature.

**Paragraph 2:** The speaker herself lives in permanent (aural) awareness of the war but it appears no-one else does (*¿por qué no escucháis?*). In the second sentence she moves from the sense of hearing to that of sight. She tears the night (*desgarro la noche*) with her wakeful eyes. At night, she feels herself to be in solidarity with all those others who live *en la oscuridad doliente*. Her eyes in the morning, having harvested the splendour of all these constantly watching eyes (*el resplandor sostenido*), will be flowers, reflecting the value of this nocturnal solidarity.

Her living blood (*circulación*) is contrasted to the body fluids of the dead lying in the earth (*los zumos que socavan la tierra de tumbas*). The *zumos* of the dead undermine the burial ground, causing it to sink down as the bodies rot among the roots (*raíces*). Thus far, the imagery refers back to Poem I. Now, she explains that she has *sangre de cirios*, blood tainted by burning candles, on her lips. These are votive candles which in a time long since forgotten (*que el pasado olvidó*), literally forgotten even by the past, burnt on altars to gods with tragic destinies (*imposibles altares de nubes a dioses de trágico sino*). The *nubes* might refer to clouds of incense burnt in honour of the gods, *imposibles* because these altars may only have existed in legend. However, it is not completely unthinkable that the invocation of gods with a tragic destiny (*sino*) might also include Christ and his bloody end on the cross, even though that would presuppose a far from orthodox interpretation of the Crucifixion, one in which the certainties of Christianity were negated, in fact. The speaker endures all this because of the boys and men tearing themselves in an arterial (relating to blood) buzzing (*que se rajan en arteriales zumbidos*) beneath the ground. The sinister buildings of sorrow (*los edificios siniestros del llanto*) which are on top of this place of death may, on one level, be construed as tombs and niches in graveyards, where the dead boys and men are buried. On another, they may be, in a more abstract sense, the sinister institutions and factions which are engaged in the war and therefore bring about such suffering and sorrow. Thus, these *edificios siniestros* may be said to take the place or offer an ironic contrast with a past in which there were *imposibles altares de nubes a dioses de trágico sino*. There is a sense that all religion has been forgotten in the carnage.

**Paragraph 3:** As the speaker sees it, she and the dead are alone in their awareness of their situation. She is also aware that this might not be obvious from her physical appearance. Even though her skin may appear sun-kissed (*mi frente sea de sol maduro*) and her hair healthy and reach up to the sky from its roots (*mis cabellos suban en raíces al cielo*), no-one should doubt the internal anguish (*angustia*) in which both her body and her soul are dying.

violencia del odio
y muerte interna

# Poem XIII

Los de acá no volveremos a oír el silencio que navegaba las noches, ni la más densa noche podrá oírse su propia campana corpórea... ¿Cómo pudieron empapar de tanta sangre la cueva de frescores de donde surtían las noches?

¡Ay, que ya no podrán vulnerarse los bosques ni captarse aves para mensajes a estrellas!

El grito de millares de gargantas, el hondo, repicador, tenebroso grito mismo, lo ha taladrado todo: noche, fragancia, y este cuenco de vientre que soñaba ser cuna.

## Commentary

**Paragraph 1:** Here again, the sense of hearing is paramount. Those of us who are here (*los de acá*) probably refers to the place in which she finds herself, in Poem XII, accompanying the dead. In this place which only she and they understand or have access to, in which they are isolated (*cuán solos estamos los muertos y yo*), they will never again hear the silence which voyaged through the night (*el silencio que navegaba las noches*). It is, of course, an oxymoron to suggest that silence may be listened to, a contradiction in terms. Then there is a conflation of night and body as she states that not even the densest night will be able to listen to the beat of its own bodily bell, meaning its heart (*oírse su propia campana corpórea*). The implication is that this silence has been shattered forever by the noise of war.

The transgressors referred to in ¿*cómo pudieron empapar de tanta sangre?* are those prosecuting the war, not those dying in droves as a result of it. They have destroyed that fresh place, a cave of cool (refreshing) air (*cueva de frescores*) from which the night spang up.

**Paragraph 2:** The imagery in this line evokes the exquisite, exotic and vaguely neo-classical paradise of *modernista* poetry. The influence of Juan

Ramón Jiménez is inescapable here. The use of this imagery is deliberately poignant in that it hearkens back to a time, not that long ago, when poets could dream of these impossible paradises and readers enjoy reading the resulting poetry. The woods can no longer be wounded (*ya no podrán vulnerarse*), that is pierced by beauty; birds can no longer be captured in order to send messages to the stars (*captarse aves para mensajes a estrellas*). This is a reference to birdsong, the same beauty which would once have pierced the woods.

**Paragraph 3:** Instead of beautiful birdsong rising to the stars there is the deep, ringing, dark roar of millions of throats (*el hondo, repicador, tenebroso grito*) and it has drilled through everything (*lo ha taladrado todo*). It has drilled through the night and the fragrances which would, for example, be associated with it in the *modernista* paradise of the previous line. It has also drilled through the speaker's own womb, which she describes as a hollow (*cuenco*) which once dreamt of becoming a cradle (*cuna*). This is a cradle which, as she states in Poem IX (*Cierto que yo no pariré hijo*), will remain unfilled while the war still rages.

Md.

# Poem XIV

Salieron todas las voces desbandadas; las empolvadas viejas voces que se guardaban en los odres del espantoso silencio, y las muchedumbres se dislocaron de llantos sobre la atezada carne de la guerra.

Mujeres cuyas raíces estaban secas, con otras desarraigadas, con muchas más investidas de duelo, gritaron al hijo desde todos los cruces del viento con el terror.

Los hombres que derramaban sus huesos cantando al frenesí hicieron con sus brazos que el sol eludiera lumbre.

Solamente los pensativos, las madres, las novias, todas las gentes de adolescencia bruñida, inevaporable, podían sonreír en medio de la muerte.

Y yo busco en mi oído la espiga de una voz que nunca se apague, que sobresalte a la eternidad.

## Commentary

**Paragraph 1:** The voices which emerge here are compared to old wine which has been kept a long time in wineskins (*odres*). The voices are so old they are covered in dust (*empolvadas*) and they emerged disjointed, scattered (*desbandadas*) from where they were once all grouped together in the same confined space. The wineskins belong to horrified silence (*espantoso silencio*) but they are no longer able to contain the sound of the voices. Every single, last one (*todas*) has come out and they made up separate crowds (*muchedumbres*) which spread out (*se dislocaron*) over the bronzed (*atezada*) flesh of war (*carne de guerra*). While *atezada* is normally a positive term indicating a healthy tan, here is it more likely to indicate the colour of flesh which is now rotting and discoloured. *Dislocarse* may also have a connotation of to drive mad or be driven mad, so the sense is that the groups which have spewed out of the wineskins have been partly or wholly separated out because they have been driven mad.

**Paragraph 2:** The women who emerge are already like plants with dried-up roots (*cuyas raíces estaban secas*) and with some roots sticking up into the air, divorced from the earth (*desarraigadas*). The majority of these womens' roots, however, are loaded with grief (*investidas de duelo*). All they can do is cry out to their (dead) sons and they do this from every single crossroads (*cruces*) where the wind and terror meet. The use of *investir*, which is normally used for honours or offices of state, adds cruel irony to the description of these women's dried-up, ungrounded roots. A crossroads would normally be a site of pleasant and useful encounters; now it is a place where wind and terror intersect.

**Paragraph 3:** The men spilled their bones (*derramaban sus huesos*). Just as the women's roots are dried-up, the men, being dead, only have their skeletons left to pour out while they sing in a frenzy (*cantando al frenesí*). As they emerge, they use their arms (*brazos*) to make sure that the sun eludes (*eludiera*) lumbre. In Poem XII *la esférica lumbre estallada de la tierra* refers to the light of an explosion. Perhaps in some sense the dead men are using their arm-bones to protect the sun from the light produced by explosions.

**Paragraph 4:** There is a suggestion here that only those who are reflective or thinkers, those who are mothers (of children who are alive), girlfriends, those in the full bloom of adolescence, are somehow protected from the reality of war and can smile in the middle of it, perhaps because they have not, as yet, been touched by it.

**Paragraph 5:** In this last line, the speaker searches for a very different intimation to those which emerged from the wineskins clamouring in grief. *Una espiga* is an ear of wheat, the part of the plant which is harvested and used to produce flour. She is looking for a voice, like this, full of potential. It will be a voice which will never go silent, which will in fact take eternity by surprise (*sobresaltar*). She does not hope to find this voice in the dystopia of suffering she has just described, she hopes instead to find it in her own ear (*en mi oído*), perhaps as a kind of prophecy or mystical insight.

# Poem XV

Llegaos a nosotros, los vivos cínicamente vivos, y anegadnos en la sangre de nuestros cuerpos despojados de lumbre.

Vosotros, los muertos en esta brutal guerra de progreso, venid a golpear nuestra sensibilidad ajena a todo, olvidada, florecida en lo augusto suyo único.

Tendremos terror de que vengáis asordando la tierra en alarido, y huiremos sin poder ir a la vida, enlosados de muerte. Porque es verdad que mientras las llagas de la pólvora se abrían el camino de vuestros vientres, todos bebíamos y sonreíamos dichosos en el sol también ajeno.

Asco hemos de darnos por vivir más que vosotros, avenida y avenida, alameda y alameda de estallados hijos.

## Commentary

**Paragraph 1:** *Los vivos cínicamente vivos* are those who live in awareness of the horrors of war. They contrast to those mentioned in Poem XIV who can smile *en medio de la muerte* because they seem innocent of its ravages. The speaker is calling on the dead, the *vosotros, los muertos*, of the next paragraph, to come and overwhelm (drown) these *cínicamente vivos*, of whom she herself is one, in the blood of their own bodies (*anegadnos en la sangre*). Their bodies may have blood coursing in them, but they are stripped of light (*despojados de lumbre*). *Lumbre* here is a more neutral term, indicating light in the positive sense.

**Paragraph 2:** She wants the dead to come and somehow knock (*venid a golpear*) the *cínicamente vivos* into a more immediate awareness of the war. She specifies it as *esta brutal guerra de progreso*, a combination of adjectives (*brutal, de progreso*) which carries heavy irony. She describes these *cínicamente vivos* as having a sensibility which is removed from everything (*ajena a todo*), which reflects the tastes of a now forgotten age (*olvidada*), which has bloomed (*florecida*) in a sense of its own august (majestic and important) uniqueness (*florecida en lo augusto suyo único*).

**Paragraph 3:** These *cínicamente vivos* appear, nonetheless, to be stuck in a place partway between life and death. They are themselves paved over with death (*enlosados de muerte*) and will not be able to flee in the direction of life if these hordes of dead, of whom they are terrified, rush towards them, rendering the earth deaf with their clamour (*asordando la tierra en alarido*).

Their terror may come from guilt, an acceptance that they were busy enjoying themselves while the dead were being slaughtered. At that time, *bebíamos y sonreíamos dichosos en el sol*. This was, of course, a *sol también ajeno*, indicating that the world in which the *cínicamente vivos* enjoyed themselves was different from the everyday world the dead would have lived in when they were alive. The dead have been killed by wounds caused by gunpowder (*las llagas de la pólvora*) which opened paths into their abdomens (*el camino de vuestros vientres*). Here the word *vientre* is used in reference to the male abdomen, as distinct from the female womb.

**Paragraph 4:** Now all that is left is for the *cínicamente vivos* to be disgusted at themselves for outliving the fallen, who fell on urban avenues (*avenidas*) and more suburban or rural roads (*alamedas*). The dead are all *hijos estallados*. These last two words draw the poem poem back to the theme of maternity dispossessed by ordnance. These were once the sons of now childless women, blown up by bombs, shells and gunfire.

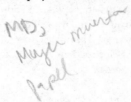

# Poem XVI

¿Y qué puedo yo hacer por vosotros? Decídmelo.

El Mar me dio su orden exacta, incorporándose mis ojos en dos barcas de quillas redondas. Me la dio el Viento, adueñándose de mis cabellos para extenderlos en rubio pañuelo de olor. La recibí de la Tierra, creciéndome, columnas de mis piernas arriba, con un estremecimiento inextinguible y frutal. ¡Todos los que mandan, hasta el Fuego, me han dicho ya lo que quieren de mí!

...¿Y nada diréis vosotros, los que descuaja el huracán del odio?

¡Cierto que sólo tengo una voz, esta voz velada calientemente, con la que poderos servir de intermediaria!

## Commentary

There is a dedication in brackets (J.R.J.) at the bottom of the page in Conde's autograph manuscript.

**Paragraph 1 (line):** Here, as in paragraph 4, she addresses all those, unlike the *cínicamente vivos* of Poem XV and those innocents in Poem XIV who can smile in the midst of war, who have been directly affected by it. In the next paragraph, she recieves instructions from the four elements: Water, Air, Earth and Fire, in that order.

**Paragraph 2:** The sea is *el mar* here, masculine and businesslike. It has given her a precise command (*orden exacta*) as a result of which her eyes have become (*incorporándose*) like two small boats (*barcas*) with round keels (*quillas redondas*). These small boats contrast with the *barcos de ébano furibundo* of Poem I or the *barco con el más esbelto pabellón de sonrisas* of Poem III.

The wind issued a second order. As it did so it took hold of her hair (*adueñándose*) and spread it in a golden sheet in the air. This echoes the reference to her hair in Poem XII, *cabellos [que suban] en raíces al cielo*.

More precisely, in this instance, it evokes one of the great Renaissance images of female beauty: Botticelli's *Birth of Venus* (*c*.1482–1486) which depicts the goddess emerging naked from an oyster shell, her golden hair floating about her, caught in the breeze. In this poem, the hair forms a *rubio pañuelo de olor*, so it has olfactory as well as visual qualities, reminiscent of the *fragancia* of Poem XIII.

She receives a third instruction from the Earth. It causes her legs to extend up into columns (*creciéndome, columnas de mis piernas arriba*) and she experiences a shudder of growing pain as this happens (*estremecimiento inextinguible y frutal*). This pain will not be extinguished (*inextinguible*) and it will bear fruit (*frutal*).

She receives a final commission, which she does not specify, from the fourth element, Fire.

**Paragraph (line) 3:** She asks those uprooted (*los que descuaja)* by the hurricane of hatred (*el huracán del odio*) if they have any task for her. It is probably a question which will not receive a reply. The form she uses (*¿y nada diréis?*) implies the absence of a response.

**Paragraph (line) 4:** In this absence, the speaker declares her intention to be their intermediary (*serviros de intermediaria*). Her voice, the only one she has at her disposal, is *velada*, veiled, but warmly so (*calientemente*) and she will use it to give expression to their suffering. In a more abstract sense, this is a statement of the public function of the poet in time of war, to be the voice of the voiceless, to utter the unutterable.

*papel*

# Poem XVII

¡Cuántas horas se oye el andar hundidor y hendidor de millares y millares de hombres que caminan la tierra desmedida del llanto!

El suelo se estremece, callándolo. El cielo se desgaja, subiéndose más alto de sí. Solamente el corazón de los anhelantes acompasa su deshielo con el rítmico sin fin de los que andan.

¿Adónde vais, hermanos de la incansable búsqueda? ¿Qué planeta de fibras, de vísceras, de miembros intocables e inmortales, queréis hallar? ¿Cómo mi sangre solitaria os escucha, os sigue, para esa armonía soñada que no oiremos jamás ninguno!

Zanjas, abismos, tajos, abren los pasos herméticos, cifras exactas de la soledad desolada... ¿Podría ver alguien un arroyo dulce entre las tierras abiertas por el Dolor..., un lucero en los cielos negros..., un alba de rubio sonreír iluminado?

## Commentary

**Paragraph 1:** The *millares y millares de hombres que caminan* may on one level evoke the sound of marching armies, on another the footsteps of the thousands of dead. The land of grief (*tierra del llanto*) across which they walk so noisily is excessively proportioned (*desmedida*). In other words, there is vastly more suffering in the world because of the war. The noise these marching men make is *hundidor y hendidor*: it causes sinking and splitting, an assonance almost exists in the similarity of the two words where only the initial vowel is different.

**Paragraph 2:** The land shudders (*el suelo se estremece*) and in doing so, silences the sound of the splitting, sinking march *(callándolo)*. The sky breaks loose (*el cielo se desgaja*), as if it had a point of anchorage from which to release itself, and rises up further than it ought to be (*más alto de sí*). Only the hearts of those who are suffused with longing (*el corazón de los anhelantes*) is able to tolerate this sound. Since *los anhelantes* are one body of sufferers, the speaker describes them as having one heart or one heartbeat. This heart is able to stay in step (*acompasa*), keep to the eternal rhythm of the marching men (*el rítmico sin fin de los que andan*). The heartbeat is a *deshielo*, a kind of thawing, brought about perhaps by at last establishing a longed-for contact of sorts with the dead.

**Paragraph 3:** The speaker asks the marching men where they are going, and addresses them as her brothers, brothers engaged in a tireless search. She wants to know which planet made of *fibras* (in this sense, muscles), entrails or guts (*vísceras*) and untouchable, eternal limbs (*miembros intocables e inmortales*) they are looking for.

She emphasises how closely her own solitary blood is listening to the sound of their marching (*¡cómo mi sangre solitaria os escucha!*) and follows their sound in the futile hope of recovering a lost, dreamt-of harmony (*para esa armonía soñada*). This harmony echoes the *tácitas armonías* of Poem VIII and the birdsong (*aves para mensajes a estrellas*) of Poem XIII.

**Paragraph 4:** Trenches (*zanjas*), chasms (*abismos*), gorges (*tajos*), great wounds in the earth open the way for hermetic steps. These steps constitute the exact cyphers (or images) of the desolate solitude (*cifras exactas de la soledad desolada*). Hermetic knowledge is that which is difficult to access without very specialised, esoteric information. Its use here suggests Juan Ramón Jiménez, yet again, symbolist poetry in general, and the early poetry of Juan Ramón in particular. *La soledad desolada* might be said to offer a pendant to the title of his early collection of symbolist poems, *La soledad sonora* (1911), especially since silence has so much resonance in these poems. The lost world of the *tácitas armonías* of Poem VIII might easily be that portrayed in *La soledad sonora*, only now it is a desolate rather than a sonorous solitude. These great wounds in the earth are opened up by sorrow, personified here as *el Dolor*.

The final despairing sequence of three questions underlines the desolation of the landscape. The answer is that no-one can find a sweet-water stream (*arroyo dulce*), a bright star (*lucero*) in the dark heavens, a dawn lit up by a golden smile (*alba de rubio sonreír iluminado*).

# Poem XVIII

Se empezaron a doler las tumbas con los quejidos de las madres parturientas. Porque se abrían desgarradas entrañas cuyos frutos costara desprender en el cuerpo a cuerpo con la eternidad. ¿Quién no tenía una tumba florida de manos rotas; quién no llevaba rosas para la sangre derramada en charcas negras sobre el asfalto, rosa de incendios?

¡Incendio, también, de tumbas en la noche sin orilla de la inmensa Noche del Duelo de las Esferas! Todas ardían, teas de muertos verdes de vida, para llanto inacabable de los hombres por nacer.

Mi hermano está hecho pavesa debajo del jardín donde pintó su primera nube, y mi hermana llora a un hombre sobre la tierra donde yo tengo hincadas las plantas que sustenta mi voz.

¿Quién podría hundir los dedos ávidos en la carne de la tierra y desgranársela ajena, como pan seco?

## Commentary

**Paragraph 1:** The tombs of the dead are conflated with the wombs of mothers giving birth (*madres parturientas*). The moaning (*los quejidos*) of mothers as they give birth is causing pain (*se empezaron a doler*) in the tombs. The torn insides (*desgarradas entrañas*, the womb and birth canal) of the women are engaged in hand-to-hand combat (*el cuerpo a cuerpo*) with eternity. It will be difficult for these *desgarradas entrañas* to surrender (*deprender*, to set loose) their fruit. The act of surrender may be the initial one to death, or a subsequent one, the release of the soul of the dead into eternity.

The *quién* in this question encompasses all those who have lost loved ones through violence, where the bodies have been mutilated or dismembered, and where therefore the tombs rather than being adorned with flowers, are bedecked (for example) with broken hands (*florida de manos rotas*). These same bereaved (the repetition of *quién*) bring roses to dress the graves of those whose blood has been spilt in dark pools on the asphalt (*sangre derramada en charcas negras sobre el asfalto*). The rose which as a symbol of love might dress the graves, as a symbol of life might be associated with blood, is finally associated with fire (*rosa de incendios*). Where in peacetime the idea of fire (passion) in the blood would be a positive aspect of the symbolism of the rose, here the fire is the produce of the destructive force of war.

**Paragraph 2:** This *incendio* engulfs all the tombs in the night. Reference to the spheres (*las Esferas*) or planets invokes the medieval concept of the harmony of the spheres, the idea that the planets in the heavens resonated with an inaudible music the relative pitch of which was determined by the mathematical distance between them and by their movements. In poetry of the period, this *musica universalis* was often treated as if it could be heard, at least by the initiated, such as lovelorn poets. Here, instead of the harmony of the spheres, there is a *Duelo de las Esferas*, as if the vibrations of pain resonated between the planets. Two gradations of night are at play here: the immense night (*la inmensa Noche*) of the cosmos in which the *Duelo de las Esferas* exists and the much smaller-scale night on Earth which is without banks or boundaries (*la noche sin orilla*).

All the tombs were burning (*todas ardían*), like torches (*teas*). This use of *teas* might be compared to the *teas de gritos* of Poem I. Here the burning material is the dead who were green (youthful, immature) in life. All this burning will go to make up an unfinishable lament (*llanto inacabable*) for men who are yet to be born (*los hombres por nacer*). These *hombres por nacer* might be those in the world of the living yet to be born, who would mourn the dead, or the dead themselves who are being born to the *madres parturientas* of the first paragraph.

**Paragraph 3:** *Mi hermano* represents the men who die in battle, *mi hermana* the women who mourn the dead men. He has been turned into a particle of burning soot (*pavesa*) beneath the garden where (as a child) he painted his first cloud, in other words in his own land. She, alive and above ground, weeps for a dead man. The speaker, in her role as voice of the suffering people (the *intermediaria* of Poem XVI) has the soles of her feet thrust into this ground (*hincadas las plantas*). Reminiscent of her *columnas de mis piernas arriba*, the growth-spurt gift of the Earth so she could carry out its mission (in Poem XVI), this rootedness is what sustains her voice.

**Paragraph 4:** This last rhetorical question asks who could sink their eager fingers (*dedos ávidos*) into the flesh of the earth (*carne de la tierra*) and break it up into crumbs (*desgranársela*) as if it were alien (*ajena*) to them, as if it were dry bread (*pan seco*). The implication is that the earth is now made up of the flesh of the war dead. No-one ought to be unaware of this any more.

# Poem XIX

*todo pasa.*
*vida es breve*
*y puede por*
*en cualqu.*
*momento*

¡Nadie me hable ya, como si la quisiera, de la Eternidad! ¡Ninguno acuda con su imprecación ni con su oreja herida por oír lo que no soñó ni Dios mismo! He visto caer los edificios como frutas reventadas, las voces más desvencijadas se desplomaron ante mí, los seres de medio ser por mis caminos se quedaron... Y todos eran eternos, fluían incesantes desde las cuevas donde la Eternidad tañía sus arpas dislocadas. Allí aprendió mi sangre la brevedad de todo suceso.

Por este dolor que duelo, ¡nadie acuda a mi ternura hecha lágrimas desesperadas! Yo bien sé que todo es mentira en cuanto se refiere al Tiempo y al entumecido principio de su perennidad..., ¿dónde? ¿en qué ámbito? No se sabe dónde vive el eterno tiempo, y la gran criatura que lo consume como a un amante otro amante consuma.

¡Fugaz locura de que otros vengan sobre mi ser, describiéndome la hermosa perspectiva de la Eternidad! Estoy oyendo cómo sobre la tierra en que se clava mi casa caen y caen las gruesas metrallas de la muerte. Estoy oyendo cómo los que amo se alejan por donde yo no alcanzaré jamás su ires. ¡Y quién vendrá a decirme cosas de la Eternidad! Yo misma, que caigo de llanto, soy tan eterna como una brisa. Yo que veo seccionado un mundo de piedra y de carne. Yo que alcancé la manera de alargar ilusionadamente mi palabra de sangre enmarañada.

¡Eternidad! Abriré el pecho de quien venga a nombrarme el fabuloso ensueño de mi alma en chispas.

## Commentary

**Paragraph 1:** She begins with an imperative. No-one should mention Eternity to her, as if it was something to be desired (*como si la quisiera*). A good Christian ought to long for Eternity as the end to a good life which will be rewarded by being in the presence of God, in Paradise for ever. Her instruction perhaps shows impatience with an orthodoxy which preaches passive acceptance of death as the will of God. The *como si la quisiera*

85

might also imply a certain hypocrisy in the attitude of those who claim to long for Eternity.

She does not wish anyone with a curse (*imprecación*) or an ear wounded (*su oreja herida*) by hearing something not even dreamt of by God (*lo que no soñó Dios mismo*) to come near her. The implication is that none of the awfulness of the present may be attributed to the will of God. Contrary to Nationalist propaganda no curse (*imprecación*) has been imposed by God on anyone. *Imprecación* is used significantly in Poem I (*los cielos se han dejado hincar imprecaciones sombrías*) to indicate the beginning of hostilites.

She has seen buildings fall like burst fruit (*frutas reventadas*), the most rickety or dilapidated (*desvencijadas*) voices have collapsed (*se desplomaron*) in front of her, beings half in being (*seres de medio ser*) are strewn along the roads she has travelled (*por mis caminos se quedaron*). The old (*voces desvencijadas*) and the young (*seres de medio ser*) have fallen, as have the buildings which might have been expected to provide shelter. The three dots at the end of this line, forming a caesura or break before the next sentence, allow for the inclusion of unmentioned others in the list.

All these, and everyone/everything else included in the caesura, have become part of eternity (*todos eran eternos*). They flowed incessantly (*fluían incesantes*) from the caves where Eternity played (*tañía*) its harps. The adjective *dislocadas* applied to the harps hearkens back to Poem XIV, where *las muchedumbres se dislocaron de llantos*. In Poem XIV, the verb seems to carry both a spatial (scattered or dislocated) and a psychological (maddened) inference. Here the harps may be dislocated in the sense that Eternity itself has been refashioned by the context of war, and they may also be maddened by all the bloodshed. In broader terms, the idea of the cave of Eternity is a possible reference to the belief, in some forms of Neo-Platonism, that the soul had a pre-existence, within Eternity, before choosing to be born, thus the particular specification that they all flowed from the caves (*fluían desde las cuevas*), new souls on their way to death. The mention of caves is almost certainly also an allusion to Plato's allegory of the cave, where the unenlightened mind is like a prisoner in a cave who can only see the world as reflections and shadows while he has his back unwittingly turned to the bright light of the sun and reality.

The speaker claims that there (*allí*), which may mean in the caves of Eternity or on the roads she has travelled (*por mis caminos*), she learned the brevity of all things. *La brevedad de todo suceso* is a gloss for her own times of the Renaissance trope of *la brevedad de la vida*, the brevity or transience of life.

**Paragraph 2:** Part of her responsibility, as *intermediaria*, is to embody the suffering of her people (*este dolor que duelo*). However, she will not be approached (*nadie acuda*), even though what may have begun as tenderness (*ternura*) has become tears of desperation (*lágrimas desesperadas*).

She avers that the everlasting or perennial nature of time, here personified as *el Tiempo*, is nothing more than a stiff principle (*entumecido principio*), presumably meaning dry and dusty and outdated. The caesura after *perennidad* makes ready for the series of questions following it (*¿dónde? ¿en qué ámbito?*).

The great creature which consumes eternal time (*la gran criatura que lo consume*) represents death at a very basic level. Its relationship to Eternity is that of one lover to another, one in which they consume each other. In a more complex sense, the use of the term *gran criatura* may contain, in part, an allusion to the Neo-Platonic idea of the demiurge or creator. While, according to Plato, this is the benevolent deity which created the material world, a world which is essentially good, in Gnosticism, a philosophy based to a large extent on Platonic principles or the inversion of them, the opposite is held. The material world is evil and so is the Demiurge who created it. This may explain the association of the *gran criatura* here with death.

**Paragraph 3:** The speaker now returns to the instruction of the opening sentence. The others who might come (*que vengan*) to describe to her the beauty of Eternity are probably, in their swift and fleeting madness (*fugaz locura*), those of a solid and orthodox Catholic faith who can believe in a heavenly paradise in spite of the horrors of war. Returning to the Platonic allegory of the cave, perhaps these may believe themselves to be the enlightened ones who do not see the world as reflected images, who have in fact seen *la hermosa perspectiva de la Eternidad*. She, on the other hand, remains locked in the world of reflected shadows which most humans recognise as reality.

She hears how again and again the thick shrapnel (*las gruesas metrallas*) of death falls on the land into which her house is nailed (*en que se clava*). In Poem X, she describes herself as having *mi planta en el suelo*; in Poem XVI she shows how the earth grew her legs into columns (*columnas de mis piernas*); in Poem XVIII, she refers to *la tierra donde yo tengo hincadas las plantas.* Here her house is nailed to the earth on which the shrapnel falls.

The result of this is that those she loves are being taken away on a journey (*sus ires*) on which she will not be able to follow them. Therefore no-one should come and attempt to voice platitudes about eternity to her (*decirme cosas de la Eternidad*). Indeed, she who is almost collapsing with grief (*que caigo de llanto*) is actually eternal, like a breeze (*como una brisa*). She sees the world split up into little bits (*seccionado*), a world of stone and flesh (*de piedra y de carne*) as opposed to the ethereal *Eternidad*. This image perhaps recalls the *tierra desgranada, como pan seco* of Poem XVIII, which, being made of the flesh of the dead, none should be able to touch.

Her word is tangled up (*enmarañada*) in blood. It has to be if what she recounts is the destruction of war. Yet, she says that she achieved a way of lengthening her word (*alcancé la manera de alargar mi palabra*). This refers back to her claim to be as eternal as a breeze, because she bears witness to the mutual devouring of death and eternity, so the *palabra alargada* is her poetry, her witness to war. The use of the adverb *ilusiona-damente* to describe how she achieved this may be an ironic comment on her inevitable disillusionment, or perhaps it indicates that she initially thought, at some level, that poetry would be a salvation.

**Paragraph 4:** In this last paragraph, she addresses Eternity directly. She will split open the chest of anyone (*abriré el pecho de quien venga*) who comes to remind her of eternity. Now it is no more than the fabulous dream of her soul (*el fabuloso ensueño de mi alma*). This dream may have been, in its time, for her also the orthodox religious belief in the eternity of the pious soul, forever in the presence of God which she rejects so vehemently in the rest of the poem, or, since the speaker has just referred specifically to her poetry, the more Romantic conception of eternity as the eternally beautiful, the source of poetic inspiration. Now all this is gone up in smoke (*chispas* are sparks, *en chispas* may indicate *el ensueño de mi alma* reduced to smoke and sparks) and the speaker's anger and bitterness are palpable.

# Poem XX

¡Selvas de nuestros jóvenes muertos! ¡Espesura del duelo que agita sus crines de gritos! Con la mano sobre el corazón me conjuráis a la vida.

¡No hay muerte, sino arboleda profusa de esperanza! ¡No hay muerte, aunque caiga la juventud bajo los hachazos de los cañones!

Los hombres no causan la muerte, los hombres no mueren nunca por ellos mismos. Es que la muerte recorre insensata las hectáreas de vientres ajados exprimiéndoles la memoria de los hijos.

Y muchos hombres se duermen en los umbrales de llanto; ésos son los que parecen muertos. Pero los que atienden, los que braman su encendido celo de vida, son los que avanzan siempre, los que penetran las densidades de la tierra, los que derraman el mañana, los que triunfarán, sabiendo morir, de la muerte.

## Commentary

**Paragraph 1:** The speaker calls out to the the forests (*selvas*) of dead young men. She hears them as a thickness (*espesura*) of pain which shakes its manes (*crines*) of cries. *Crin* may also mean esparto grass. *Crines* are first invoked in Poem VII, on the *corceles de ébano del duelo*. Here the *selvas de nuestros jóvenes muertos* summon her (*me conjuráis*) to life. She has her hand on her heart (*con la mano sobre el corazón*) as this happens to her.

**Paragraph 2:** For the first time, the speaker introduces a sliver of hope. After the absolute desolation of her denial of Eternity in the previous poem, this is a turning point. There is no death, only a path, profuse with (trees of) hope (*arboleda profusa de esperanza*). At this remove, it may perhaps be possible to suspect that this has been engendered from the *alma en chispas* of Poem XIX. Even if the young fall beneath the axe blows (*hachazos*) of field artillery (*cañones*) she repeats that there is no death.

**Paragraph 3:** However, the reason why there is no death appears to be based on a casuistry and an unconvincing one at that. Men do not kill themselves, death happens because death itself runs around hectares of worn-out wombs (*vientres ajados*), squeezing from them the memory of the children they bore (*exprimiéndoles la memoria de los hijos*). Death is senseless, feelingless while it does this (*insensata*). The effect of this attempt to exonerate men from blame is to render the plight of the women who lose their children even more poignant. As the next paragraph shows, men have a choice, to be passive cowards or active heroes; women have none.

**Paragraph 4:** In this paragraph, she elaborates a complex comparison between two ways of dying. Some men just appear to sleep in the shadows of grief (*los umbrales del llanto*). They only appear to be dead (*parecen muertos*). Her implication, later on, seems to be that these men have not struggled either to live or to die well. Others however, those who pay attention (*los que atienden*), those who roar (*braman*) their fiery lust (*su encendido celo*) for life, will always go forward. They will penetrate the depths of the earth, they will pour forth the morning (*derraman el mañana*). *El mañana* indicates the future in an abstract sense. These men will triumph over death because they have known how to die, presumably because they have died bravely.

# Poem XXI

Es el tiempo maduro de llorar. Unánimes, todas las madres visten sus crespones nocturnos. Las alcobas se partieron como frutas podridas, y las mujeres jóvenes olvidaron sus senos. Vino la voz de alboroto de la guerra.

Es el día de mirar al mar sin entender su movimiento de relojería. Es el tiempo de apagar lámparas y pájaros. Es el día de cabalgar una escucha perenne, enlutada.

Apretadas de martirio, las madres se miran los cuerpos, las manos y los ojos deshabitados.

## Commentary

**Paragraph 1:** Now the time is ripe for mourning (*el tiempo maduro de llorar*). The women all in unanimity (*unánimes*) wear black mourning ribbons (*crespones*); these were usually attached to a hat or other head-dress, or, for example, to a flag. Here they are described as being *nocturnos*, adding a further dimension to their blackness. Their bedrooms (*alcobas*) are now split open (*se partieron*) like rotten fruit and the young women, who should be nursing babies, have forgotten that they have breasts (*olvidaron sus senos*). This is because the noise of the commotion (*la voz de alboroto*) of war has come upon them.

**Paragraph 2:** This is a day to gaze upon the sea without understanding its clock-like movement (*su movimiento de relojería*). Not only lights but birds must also be extinguished. The mention of *pájaros* here recalls the *aves para mensajes a estrellas* of Poem XIII; ordinarily they might be expected to produce music, here they must be doused like lamps. Instead, a permanent lookout (*escucha perenne*) must be posted, one who will ride about (*cabalgar*) constantly, one who will be dressed in mourning (*enlutada*).

**Paragraph 3:** For their part, the women will be held tight by martyrdom (*apretadas de martirio*); in pleasanter circumstances *apretadas* might describe the feel of tight-fitting clothes. These women will look at their own or each other's bodies, hands and eyes and find them uninhabited (*deshabitados*). It is worth noting that the *cuerpo deshabitado* is a recurring image in Rafael Alberti's cubist *Sobre los ángeles* (1929); however, the sense of being *deshabitado* here probably relates specifically to these women's lost or unengendered sons.

# Poem XXII

Nadie sabe dónde está la luz. Y van los hombres con las manos extendidas, altas las frentes y una esperanzada sonrisa en los labios fríos. Las mujeres aguardan con sus pupilas agrandadas por el deseo, en cualquier nube, umbral o isla...¡ Solamente yo soy el ser que sí conoce su luz!

¿No la veis, los que ahincosamente miráis, sobresaltarme como una corriente, escapárseme de las sienes, cabellos y hombros? ¡Iluminaremos el mundo sin voz de vuestra búsqueda!

Estoy encendida, sí; encendida de mediodía exacto, de tarde cumplida. Y mi fe en mi luz es mi única lumbre. *esperanza*

Aprended todos de mí a llevar muy en pie la llama. *poeta vate/ profeta*

## Commentary

**Paragraph 1:** The speaker begins by describing the search for light; the men seem to look upwards, with hopeful smiles (*una sonrisa esperanzada*). At this stage, they might be looking for some sort of conventional divine apparition or omen. The pupils (*pupilas*) of the women's eyes have been widened (*agrandadas*) by desire for this light, and they look for it in any cloud, threshold (a door marking a place of entry or some other kind of boundary) or island (*cualquier nube, umbral o isla*). Then with the caesura after *isla* comes the punchline, as it were, heightened by exclamation marks. The speaker is the only one who knows the truth about the light: that each person possesses their own, it does not come from the heavens or any external source.

**Paragraph 2:** She asks the diligently (*ahincosamente*) searching people if they cannot see her light escaping from her temples, her hair, her shoulders (*de las sienes, cabellos y hombros*). *Sobresaltarme como una corriente* suggests that this light is a strong current, like a tidal wave washing over and beyond her. She believes that with this light, perhaps with their light too, if they could identify it, they might be able to light up the world of

*vza las* (handwritten annotation)
*omJvRg*

their search (*iluminaremos el mundo ... de vuestra búsqueda*). This world is not only deficient in light, it also appears to have no voice (*el mundo sin voz de vuestra búsqueda*). She has already proposed herself as their voice (Poem XVI); now she is offering to be their light, or help them find their own.

**Paragraph 3:** She explains that she is lit up like midday (*mediodía exacto*), when the sun is at its highest and the day at its brightest, and the end of the evening (*tarde cumplida*), when the sunset is at its most colourful, just before the sun slips below the horizon. She insists that she has faith in her light (*luz*) which in turn is her only *lumbre*, a warmer kind of light, such as that which comes from fire, a consolation in other words and the only one she has.

**Paragraph 4:** *Luz* and *lumbre* here become *llama*, like the flame carried in a torch. She tells the people to learn from her how to carry their flame with purpose (*llevar muy en pie*). Inevitably, this may draw comparison with the type of torchlight procession favoured in fascist, and even non-fascist, pageantry at the time, with the contrast between such an employment and the desolation of these lost and dispossessed rendered even more acute.

# Poem XXIII

¿Quién cree en mí? ¿Quién cree en los que mueren? ¿Quién cree en la misma fe de los que van a morir?

¡Temblad aquellos que vivís ajenos a la contienda inmensa donde cada muerto es un retroceso de la vida y un adelantado del ensueño!

No se promueve la muerte a marejadas sin que los montes alivien su espesor. No se desgarran los vientres sin que el aire no queme estertores. No muere un solo hombre sin que crezca una responsabilidad trágica en los que perviven.

¡Atended el legado de los muertos, hombres fríos y ajenos: se os deja la vida, la intacta vida vertical, para que proscribáis definitivamente la muerte!

## Commentary

**Paragraph 1:** Here the related concepts of faith and belief link back to the previous poem where the speaker states that her faith in her light will be enough to guide the lost and the searching. Faith and belief are spread wider in this poem, from the speaker to the dead, to those who are about to die. Her question asks, indirectly perhaps, what those about to die believe in.

**Paragraph 2:** As ever, she warns those who attempt to insulate themselves from the reality of war (*los que vivís ajenos* (distant/removed) *de la contienda*) to be fearful, as if their fate will, ultimately, be worse than anyone else's. Each death is a pulling backwards (*retroceso*) of life, a moving forwards (*adelantado*) of death. She uses *el ensueño* here, though it normally means dream or fantasy, in place of death, much as sleep and dreaming have been associated with death since Poem I where the speaker describes herself as having a dream of death in common with the dead (*pues ellos y yo tenemos igual designio de ensueño debajo de la tierra*).

**Paragraph 3:** The swell or surge of rough seas (*marejadas*) is used in Poem X, in the phrase which provides the title of the entire sequence (*¿cómo puedo gozarlo* [*el sueño*] *mientras los hombres mueren a marejadas?*). This death coming on in waves will not be stirred up (*no se promueve*) without the mountains thinning out their own thickness (*sin que ... alivien su espesor*) in response, perhaps by incorporating the bodies of the dead into their mass.

The tearing (*desgarrar*) of wombs in the act of giving birth, as in the *desgarradas entrañas* of Poem XVIII, will inevitably lead to death rattles (*estertores*) burnt by/in the air. Here again she engages in sensory conflation (synaesthesia), with the sound of the death rattles expressed as a tactile/visual phenomenon (burning).

The culmination of this rhetorical sequence of three consequences is the responsibility which inevitably falls on the survivors (*los que perviven*). This is perhaps the explanation of her warning to those removed from the conflict (*aquellos ... ajenos a la contienda*) in the previous paragraph.

**Paragraph 4:** These survivors (*hombres fríos y ajenos*, repeating the use of *ajeno* from the second paragraph) are addressed in this last line. They have inherited a legacy (*legado*) from the dead and retain, in contrast to the dead and buried, *la intacta vida vertical*. Her hope in them is almost the only thing which makes war endurable, and she expects them to carry out the obligation put on them by the dead to proscribe death, in other words to put an end to war forever. An aspiration which is all the more poignant for its impossibility.

# Poem XXIV

Nos derramaron los odres de las sombras. En vano quiero alumbrar. Hay tanta sombra que la luz se encoge hasta limitarse a mi cuerpo.

Los campos se volcaron de sus campanas de agua; los sembrados irguieron flores negras. Todo caminó sombrío por las cuestas del Alba y por los llanos de la Noche.

Mi dolor oscuro tenía tres alas lentas. De nadie era la mano que ordeñaba leche negra para rebaños agonizantes. De todos eran los pies que crujían las rebanadas del suelo seco de luz.

¡Ved mi llama, acercaos a mi lumbre! Soy un grito que el fuego dejó entre vosotros los que odiáis la Primavera, y arderé hasta incendiaros los ojos.

## Commentary

**Paragraph 1:** Shadows have been poured over the speaker and her people as if out of wineskins (*odres*). She who is the light, maybe even the prophet leading her people in the wasteland, finds that the shadow has forced the light to shrink back (*se encoge*) to the confines of her body.

**Paragraph 2:** Agriculture is in a state of inversion. The fields have cast themselves out of the irrigation bells (*se volcaron de sus campanas de agua*). In the normal state of things, water from irrigation channels would be poured on the fields from the *campanas*, water-carrying, bell-shaped vessels used in the traditional irrigation systems of Valencia and Andalusia put in place under Muslim rule. In the same vein, the planted fields (*los sembrados*) have produced or erected (*irguieron*) black flowers. No matter whether it is night or day, all is moved sombrely (*sombrío*) along hills (*cuestas*) and plains (*llanos*).

**Paragraph 3:** The inverted world continues here. Her pain had three wings; the symbolism of three is not explicitly explained: the reference could be religious (the Trinity) or human (mind/body/heart). Suffering, dying herds (*rebaños agonizantes*) were being milked (*ordeñar*) by an unknown hand, producing black milk. The land in this dystopia is dessicated so that everyone's feet crunch (*crujir*) as they walk on strips (*rebanadas*) of land, dried out because they are starved of light, not water.

**Paragraph 4:** The speaker returns to her role as prophet and embodiment of saving light. She points out, in the first paragraph, that there is just enough left. She describes herself as a cry (*un grito*) left among them, perhaps overlooked by *el fuego*, the destructive fire of war. She identifies her people, in this inverted world, as hating the Spring, but she will herself burn (*arderé*) until their eyes light up (*hasta incendiaros los ojos*).

# Poem XXV

Hay soledad en el dolor de explosión. Hasta los seres que se juntan despavoridos están solos, y los que están solos se cimbrean como troncos desnudos a los que azotara un tifón. Nadie está si no es consigo en el momento del espanto.

Solamente cuando yo me apretaba contra ti, madre, en aquellas noches inmensurables de miedo, estaban unidos todos, absolutamente todos los que aman el mundo.

No esta madrugada de chirriantes estallidos, entre cuyas trizas he alzado mi voz pidiendo compañía infructuosamente. Mi soledad hasta la luna me marca en las paredes letras de fuego, que gritan verdades estridentes a mi alma, mientras las bombas caen podridas, en racimos, por los alrededores de mi angustia.

## Commentary

**Paragraph 1:** This is, in many ways, the most intimate and personal of the poems in the sequence. Conde speaks a little more directly than is her wont of her own experience of bombardment and provides an insight into how that experience extrapolated, in her poetry, into the creation of a speaker–figure whose role of voice/light/prophet develops as the sequence moves along. She meditates on the solitude of fear. Even those who cling together in terror (*se juntan despavoridos*) are essentially alone. Those who are actually as well as metaphorically alone in a state of terror must sway (*cimbrearse*) like naked tree trunks (*troncos desnudos*) whipped (*azotar*) by a typhoon (*tifón*). The interplay of *ser* and *estar* in *nadie está si no es consigo* emphasises the existential aloneness of fear, at the moment of horror (*espanto*) even huddled in the midst of other people.

**Paragraph 2:** Conde admits that she found a sense of belonging only when holding her mother close on those long, immeasureable (*inmensurables*)

99

nights. Then, she felt that all those who loved the world were united together.

**Paragraph 3:** The present, however, is different. Her mother appears to be absent. The morning is full of screeching explosions (*chirriantes estallidos*), among the shreds or smithereens (*trizas*) of which she has raised her voice (*alzar la voz*) fruitlessly (*infructuosamente*) in search of the presence of others (*compañía*). Her isolation is cosmic, it reaches to the moon (*hasta la luna*) and back. This solitude is marked in letters of fire on the wall. This writing on the wall, perhaps in the concrete world the result of strafing fire from bomber aircraft, is inevitably a type of prophecy. In the Bible (Daniel 5: 25–31), writing on the wall prefigures the death of Belshazzar, king of Babylon, and the division of his kingdom among his enemies. It takes the Jewish captive Daniel, who does not belong to Belshazzar's court, to decipher writing which has defeated his court astrologers and necromancers. Here the writing is intelligible to Conde, it shouts strident truths at her (*verdades estridentes*) while the bombs fall all around, rotten (*podridas*) and in clusters (*en racimos*), like grapes.

# Poem XXVI

El día de la paz yo me sentiré perdida, asordada, deslumbrada. No conoceré a ninguno, ni siquiera tendré cerca a quien hoy conozco más que a mi sangre, porque la paz dilatará todos los aires y en ellos se perderán los seres buscándose, alejándose de las cercanías que en la guerra anudaron.

Sola, deshabitada, iré por la paz llorándola y llorándome, pues olvidé el sosiego, la seguridad, las serenidades; y como, súbitamente, me lo interrumpirán todo —aviones, cañonazos, gritos de horror—, no sabré qué hacer con mi libertad (¿para quién?) ni con mi sosiego...

¡Acérquese la Paz, vénganos el día de la paz! Aunque las madres no recobrarán a sus hijos muertos, ni los niños a sus padres, ni los ausentes a los reencontrados...

## Commentary

This poem is placed after Poem XXVII, 'Veníais a mí' in the manuscript original. (It is, however, numbered 28 in the manuscript because the manuscript original jumps from No. 21 to No. 23, probably a simple oversight.) There are two extra paragraphs in the manuscript original. See Appendix 1.

**Paragraph 1:** This poem looks forward to a day, as yet unrealised, when there will be peace. The speaker imagines herself lost, deafened (*asordada*), dazzled (*deslumbrada*) by such an eventuality. Those whom, now, she knows better than her own blood (*quien hoy conozco más que a mi sangre*; the back of one's hand in the English idiom) will inevitably become distanced. War creates intimacies of convenience, people who might never have known each other or chosen to associate together of necessity become close. Peace ruptures these associations and friendships. Here, the speaker imagines it bringing a dilation or expansion of conditions and relationships (*dilatará todos los aires*) such that people will become lost searching for those from whom they have been separated during the war, removing themselves from the closeness (*las cercanías*) cemented (*anudar*, to knot) in wartime.

**Paragraph 2:** The speaker imagines that she will be undone (*llorándola y llorándome*, weeping for the peace and weeping for herself) in these new circumstances. During the war she lost touch with her peace of mind (*sosiego*), her security (*seguridad*), her serenity (*las serenidades*), she grew accustomed to the noises of war (*aviones, cañonazos, gritos de horror*) and does not know how she will cope if they are interrupted (*me lo interrumpirán todo*). Her liberty will have no purpose in peacetime, there will be no-one to whom it will be of any use (*¿para quién?*). She has been the prophet and the light of her people in war but sees no function for herself when it is all over.

**Paragraph 3:** Yet she must, of course, welcome the coming of peace. The distinction between *la Paz* and *el día de la paz* is between the abstract ideal of Peace and the first day, of many, of peacetime. This has to be desired even though it will not bring restitution to the mothers who have lost sons, the children who have lost parents or, more cryptically, the absent (*los ausentes*) who will not recover those found again (*los reencontrados*). The absent may be the dead or those in exile, in hiding or imprisonment; *los reencontrados*, those believed lost who have been found or have found each other, but who will, nonetheless, continue to suffer the loss of the absent.

# Poem XXVII

Veníais a mí por entre las ruinas de frondosas civilizaciones, por entre las raíces de Herculano, Pompeya, Roma... Veníais a mí por debajo y por encima del mundo, y vuestros ojos y vuestras manos traían el olor de las flores petrificadas.

Yo estaba sola, olvidada de vosotros y sin saber nada de mí. Cuando os supe, primero fue a través de mapas y de láminas, y de esa bola cruzada de hilos azules que son ríos, y de morados ardidos que son mares. Nadie sabía de mí. En ningún libro, todavía, aparecía el edificio de mi inteligencia ni la pleamar de mi corazón. Seguíais viniendo; seguíais viniendo todos los que teníais derecho a creeros felices porque el mundo colgó de vuestros ojos las galerías de sus museos, de vuestros brazos el estrépito de sus trenes, y de vuestros senos, torsos, cinturas, piernas, y del ala ligera de vuestros pies el estremecimiento del amor. Y mi voz seguía más honda aún que todas las raíces de todas las ruinas, que todos los estanques donde bañaron el oro de sus estatuas los griegos y los romanos.

¡Ahora sí que también voy yo a vosotros por entre ruinas! Pero mis ruinas no tienen hiedra en sus muros, ni hay en ninguno de mis frisos galopares interrumpidos de vencedores plásticos hacia el Olimpo.

## Commentary

This is placed before XXVI, 'El día de la paz' in Conde's autograph manuscript. See note to Poem XXVI.

**Paragraph 1:** Herculaneum and Pompeii were ancient Italian towns, near present-day Naples, destroyed by the erruption of Mount Vesuvius in AD 79. The speaker describes their civilizations, along with that of Rome, as leafy (*frondosas*), probably in the sense of wealthy and cultured. The caesura which ends this opening phrase allows for the passage of time from the ancient world to the present and for a relationship between the fate of Pompeii, Herculaneum, Rome and the Civil War present to be established. The people she addresses were still coming towards her, and they had about them the odour of petrified flowers (*flores petrificadas*). Pompeii was covered in molten lava and as it cooled it petrified, that is fixed in stone, everything: people, animals, buildings, utensils.

**Paragraph 2:** The speaker first knew of the existence of the people of Pompeii and Herculaneum from maps and plates or illustrations in books (*mapas y láminas*). She located them on a ball (*bola*) crossed with blue threads (*cruzada de hilos azules*) for rivers and patches of reddish purple (*morados ardidos*) for seas, in other words a globe. In contrast, at this time, she had written nothing, nothing was known of her intelligence or the high tide (*pleamar*) of her heart. All those people coming towards her from the ancient world laid the artistic, scientific and intellectual basis on which the modern world is built. Museum galleries in which the remains of the ancient world are displayed are founded on the artistic eye of the ancient world: *el mundo colgó de vuestros ojos* (hung from your eyes) *las galerías de sus museos*. Modern transport (*el estrépito de sus trenes*) is derived from the handiwork (*el mundo colgó de vuestros brazos*) of the ancients. Even the modern appreciation of love and beauty is rooted in ancient ideals: *de vuestros senos, torsos, cinturas, piernas, y del ala ligera de vuestros pies el estremecimiento* (pleasure/sensations) *del amor*. Her voice, as she watched them come, as she fulfilled her role of prophet and voice of her people, continued on a level much deeper than all the ancient ruins (*todas las raices de todas las ruinas*) or even the pools in which the ancient Greeks and Romans doused the gold of their statues (*los estanques donde bañaron el oro de sus estatuas*), as part of the sculpting/smelting process.

**Paragraph 3:** Now she too – as a result of her giving voice to the suffering of her people, as a result of the suffering she has shared with her people – has her own ruins. Unlike those of ancient Greece and Rome, hers are recent and therefore not yet covered in ivy (*hiedra*); neither does she have architectural remains containing friezes (*frisos*), scenes on a wall in mosaic or plaster or stone carvings depicting an episode from mythology, frozen in time, the *galopares interrumpidos de vencedores plásticos hacia el Olimpo*, the interrupted (because a moment is captured in art) galloping of sculpted/crafted victors on their way to Mount Olympus (the home of the Gods in Greek mythology) to be crowned in victory.

104

# Poem XXVIII

Costado a costado, boca a boca, cuerpo a cuerpo, el Tiempo y yo esta noche nupcial de inauguración del Invierno.

Guerra. Me aprieta la sangre sus collares de venas. Guerra. Suben por mi cuerpo los pasos que dejé de andar voluntariamente. Guerra. Aprieto mis manos contra mis piernas tensas, duras y morenas. Guerra. ¡Guerra con barro, sangre, plumas de ángeles y de palomas, mantos de Mediterráneo y aleluyas de cielos dispares!

Mano a mano, nosotros, Tiempo amante, llevamos la órbita de la Guerra.

## Commentary

**Paragraph 1:** The speaker describes herself in a ritual conjugal embrace with Time, on the night of the beginning of Winter (*inauguración del Invierno*). This constitutes a wedding night (*noche nupcial*). In the Celtic calendar it is Samhain (31 October/1 November); for Catholics it is the Feast of All Souls (1 November).

**Paragraph 2:** She describes the effects war has on her body. Her blood tightens its necklaces of veins (*collares de venas*), the patterns veins make in the body; she appears to walk against her will (*suben por mi cuerpo los pasos que dejé de andar voluntariamente*); her legs are hard and tense, her fists presssing against them. All is tension. The repetition of the word *guerra* builds into a long definition. This is war with mud (*barro*), blood, the wings of angels and doves, Mediterranean cloaks (*mantos de Mediterráneo*), like/of the eponymous sea (possibly the cloak of the Virgin, Star of the Sea), alleluias emanating from skies or heavens which are uneven or do not match. Continuing the theme of sacred ritual established in the first paragraph, this middle paragraph might almost be read as a litany, listing the qualities of war, its effects on her corporeal being, the combination of human and ritual elements which make it up in this instance.

**Paragraph 3:** This last paragraph returns to the ritual conjugal relationship between the speaker and her lover, Time (*Tiempo amante*). Together (*mano a mano*, hand in hand) they sustain the orbit of war. There is possibly an implied comparison here between the act of sustaining or holding up the (circular) orbit  and the sacerdotal function of a Catholic priest in holding up the communion host either in the act of consecration during Mass or in a monstrance for other devotions. The *órbita de la guerra* is, of course, an inversion of the healing, cleansing significance of the communion host, which might be related to the black dystopia of Poem XXIV.

# Poem XXIX

Si el Viento se moja de alaridos y acorre las casas danzoras suyas, temed a los muertos.

Temed a los adolescentes caídos en las guerras sin fin de los hombres más abeles porque la tierra está repleta de ellos y los crecerá punzantes vientos.

Temamos a los que vuelven vivos de entre los muertos. A los mutilados. ¡Escóndense los sanos, los completos, porque nadie perdonará su ufanía!

Suspiran los cayentes, y el haz inmenso de sus soplos empuja la Noche, máximo navío de luto, por entre calles abiertas en mi corazón.

## Commentary

**Paragraph 1:** This marks a return to the abstract landscape of nightmare. The wind has dancing houses (*casas danzoras*) to the aid of which it rushes (*acorrer*) when it soaks itself (*mojarse*) in screams (*alaridos*). The speaker warns that when this happens the dead are to be feared.

**Paragraph 2:** These dead are the adolescent males who have fallen in the war. She categorises the war as belonging to the endless wars of *los hombres más abeles*. *Abel* may possibly relate to *bélico*, warlike or bellicose, though probably not, in this context, to Abel, the peace-loving brother of Cain. The land is full to bursting (*repleta*) with the bodies of these young men and out of them will grow (*los crecerá*) biting (*punzantes*) winds. These adolescents are therefore to be feared.

**Paragraph 3:** Her instruction changes in this paragraph, from *temed* to *temamos*. What must be feared by them and by her now are those returning from war: the *mutilated (los mutilados)* and those who are unscathed. However she instructs the unscathed (*los sanos, los completos*) to hide themselves as nobody will be able to pardon them their self-satisfaction (*ufanía*). In other words, there will be no unproblematic return from war for them either.

**Paragraph 4:** In this closing paragraph, she characterises the Night (*Noche*) as the largest of mourning ships (*máximo navío de luto*). This refers to the *barco con el más esbelto pabellón de sonrisas* of Poem III, when perhaps there was some hope that the speaker might be able to prevail against the forces of destruction. Now the sighs of the falling (*los cayentes*) are like a sheaf (*haz*) being pushed along the open streets of her heart by the Night and there is no hope.

# Poem XXX

Temíamos el Hambre, y salimos por los campos buscando con qué apaciguarla: humildes bestias, seres que las sacrificaran hallamos para nutrir aún nuestros cuerpos. Volvimos, en pleno fragor guerrero, con las cosas que nos alumbrarían parcamente el invierno. ¡Cuántas manos tendidas a nuestra fraternidad esperaban agudas!

Pero con nosotros llegó, por el aire, la muerte. Se arrojó en oleada, próvida, como si fuera ella, de tan generosa, la misma vida. Cayó sobre las casas pequeñas, sobre las locomotoras grandes, los vagones míseros, y los hombres que trajinaban su mediodía, los niños que gritaban la mañana de sol ácido, y las mujeres sufridoras de hombres y de niños...

¿Quién comería pan, cuánto pan comería ese quién si cada día la muerte arrasaba y barría el corazón de las ciudades? ¿Qué importaba el hambre si la muerte las calma todas?

Y sentimos afán de arrojar entre la chatarra el pan, los frutos, la carne que logramos para los fríos implacables, viendo a los que sólo han hecho precedernos, muertos como ovejas entre hierros, mármoles, piedras de la calle y cascotes de metralla.

## Commentary

This poem appears to narrate an actual event.

**Paragraph 1:** In wartime people are forced to eat anything they can lay their hands on, anything, as Conde states here, with which they can sate their hunger (*con qué apaciguarla*). This includes the *humildes bestias* in the countryside. These humble beasts are almost certainly not the animals raised or hunted for food in peacetime but wild animals and small rodents of a sort not usually killed and eaten by humans, or any remaining farm animals used as working beasts. The *seres que las sacrificaran* are those prepared to kill them. The use of *sacrificar* entails an element of ritual sacrifice or the sense that one good (the value of some of these *bestias* as working farm animals, perhaps) is being sacrificed to another (satisfying human hunger). As they returned to the city, amid the full roar (*fragor*) of battle, they hoped nevertheless to light up or warm (*alumbrar*) the winter, albeit frugally (*parcamente*), with the things they brought with them. This probably means they brought firewood as well as food. The last sentence of this paragraph is almost Gongoresque (Luis de Góngora, 1561–1627) in the placing of *agudas*, which qualifies the noun *manos* at the beginning of the sentence, at its end. The hands of those awaiting the return of the foragers are thin or sharp (in desperation); they are dependent on the fraternal care (*la fraternidad*) of those who were fit and able to perform this task.

**Paragraph 2:** However, the *pleno fragor guerrero* proves to be literal as well as metaphorical in this instance. As they return, the city is being bombed (*por el aire, la muerte*). The bombers (*la muerte*) come in a wave (*en oleada*), this wave (of bombers) is provident (*próvida*), except that, unlike the returning foragers who are bringing food (and firewood) to nurture life, the bombers are replete with the wherewithal of death and destruction. Conde's bitter comment, *como si fuera ella, de tan generosa, la misma vida* (as if she (*la muerte*) were life itself, in all her generosity), sums this terrible contrast up. She then lists all those different elements of the population of the city, from extreme to extreme: *locomotoras grandes* and *vagones míseros* (large train engines, miserable train carriages); men rushing about (*trajinar*) at midday, children crying in *la mañana de sol ácido*, a morning in which the sun seems acid, caused either by the season of the year, or shells raining down and *las mujeres sufridoras de hombres y niños*, long-suffering women, putting up with men and children. All these are targets. The caesura at the end leaves space to consider their fate.

**Paragraph 3:** The two rhetorical questions in this paragraph address directly the futility of struggling to remain alive when death is all around. Why would anyone eat bread (*ese quién* is a repetition of the speculative *quién* in *¿quién comería pan?*) while death is sweeping (*barrer*) and blowing away (*arrasar*) the hearts of cities? Hunger surely is not important if death calms all hungers (*las calma todas*).

**Paragraph 4:** In fact, when the foragers return with the food (*el pan, los frutos, la carne*) they have obtained in order to protect their community from the implacable cold of winter (*los fríos implacables*) and find those they left behind dead in the streets, their initial, and very human, impulse (*sentimos afán de*) is to throw their provisions onto the débris (*chatarra*) left by the bombs. The dead are now themselves like sacrificial animals, like sheep amidst the shards of metal (*hierros*) and marble (*mármoles*) from destroyed buildings, the cobbles (*piedras de la calle*) and the shrapnel and shell casings (*cascotes de metralla*). A very different harvest.

# Poem XXXI
## El héroe

¿Es que alguno de entre nosotros partió la tierra a hachazos? ¿Quién derrumbó esta corteza alzada en montes? ¿Qué brazo potente esgrimió la fuerza de Dios para combatirle a Dios su obra delirante?...

Hay entre nosotros, conmigo, junto a ti, un frénetico que se derrama como un vaso de óleo, un hombre para cuyos ojos todo cabe en un impulso y de cuyas piernas se pueden hacer columnas para la bóveda del cielo. ¿Cómo podría atreverse el cielo a caer sobre la tierra si él le hinca su cabeza para realzarlo, sujetárselo encima?

¡Hemos parido un héroe, un hombre que contiene en sí, en su sangre aprisionada, millares de seres que murieron con su locura dentro! ¡Quítensenos de ante los ojos maravillados todos los que no son aptos para desbaratar elementos!

Nos conmueve una embriaguez telúrica porque hallamos hijo nuestro al mismo Dios. El Héroe es su esencia. El Héroe es su ciencia. ¿Qué importa que su heroismo sea contra mí o a favor mío? ¿Qué importa mi muerte si quien me mata es un ciclón, un arrebato, un volcán, un océano, ¡un héroe!?

Yo quiero morir con Dios. Véngame como me venga.

¿Alguno quisiera vivir entre débiles, cobardes, aunque hermanos? ¡Yo prefiero al héroe, sea o no sea hermano! Si mío, qué gloria de admiración y de amor; si enemigo, ¡buena suerte la que den sus manos claras y verdaderas!

Un héroe es un enviado del cosmos. Si yo tengo la razón contra él y él me vence, a los dioses diremos nuestra contienda. Ahora, yo muero por él.

## Commentary

It is interesting that Conde should choose to place this paean of praise to the figure of the hero at this point in the sequence, when she has begun to anticipate defeat and the end of the war, rather than at the beginning. War poetry, certainly that of the First World War and the Spanish Civil

War, tends to begin with optimistic propaganda, exhortations to heroism and patriotic encouragement of the troops and ends in weary disillusionment and a retailing of the horrors of war. Her portrait of the hero and the identification of the speaker with the heroic nature of the hero at this late stage conveys an element of doubt as to the justice of her own cause; possibly it is a sardonic and hysterical gesture of despair and defiance at the essentially unheroic nature of what has taken place.

The glorification of the figure of the hero, a giant like Atlas full of pent-up fury against injustice but pure of intention, may be related to the fascist cult of the hero or the superman (*Übermensch*), as may scorn for those lacking in courage. However, in Conde's case the weak are exclusively those lacking in fortitude, whereas in fascism the weak encompassed all those of unsound mind or body or undesirable beliefs. In a time of war and propaganda it would have been difficult to avoid the use of such imagery, however tainted, particularly as Soviet-style communism promoted almost precisely the same type of heroic visual aesthetic as fascism. The monumental heroic figure with square jaw, huge limbs and a powerful body was prevalent in the visual art of the 1930s and the Republican government's propaganda machine adopted the iconography just as wholeheartedly as the Fascists, most notably in poster art, some of which was commissioned from the great names of the day. Here, Conde reproduces this figure in poetry and attempts to identify the hero with the essence and wisdom of God, and perhaps to isolate in the actions of a hero who is pure in heart some sense of goodness amid the strife and chaos of war.

**Paragraph 1:** The three questions in this opening paragraph make it clear that the being who split (*partir*) the land with axe blows (*hachazos*), who tore down (*derrumbar)* the tree bark (*corteza*) which had grown into (*alzada en*) mountains (mountain forests, perhaps), who was powerful enough (*qué brazo potente*) to brandish (*esgrimir*) a force equal to that of God against God and His delirium or ecstasy-inducing work (*su obra delirante*) must be extraordinary, superhuman. The caesura allows time for contemplation of this near certainty.

**Paragraph 2:** Three distinct but related locations are offered for this being: *entre nosotros, conmigo, junto a ti*, showing that this figure is everywhere and, at the same time, personally present to each individual. He is *un frenético*, in the sense of the hyperactivity of extreme emotion or motivation, who spills himself like a container of oil (*un vaso de óleo*; this is not cooking oil, *aceite*, it is rather fuel oil or therapeutic oil). He is a man in whose eyes everything may be encompassed in a single impulse. His legs are vast and strong enough to be columns which hold up the vault of the heavens (*la bóveda del cielo*). This is probably a reference to Atlas, a Titan (giant), in Greek mythology, who was at first the guardian of the pillars which were believed to hold up the sky and later, in punishment for a major transgression, obliged to hold up the sky himself. The speaker asks how it is possible that the sky could fall onto the earth if such a one drove his head into the sky (*hincar*) in order to raise it up again (*realzar*) and hold it above him (*sujetárselo encima*; *lo* refers to the sky; the reflexive *se* indicates that he grips it closely to himself in order to keep it up). There is an echo here, in the use of the word *hincar*, of the pierced skies/heavens in Poem I: *porque los cielos se han dejado hincar imprecaciones sombrías*. Indeed, the action of the hero would now constitute a form of redress if this action were not within a rhetorical question.

**Paragraph 3:** The people have finally given birth (*hemos parido*) to a hero; one who contains in himself (*en sí*), in his own imprisoned blood (*sangre aprisionada*) the thousands who died with their *locura dentro*, anger or energy or warlust which somehow was not expressed even though they died in war. The hero encapsulates in himself all this frustrated valour. This being the case, she instructs all those who are not prepared or equipped for elemental battle (*desbaratar elementos*, to disrupt or ruin the elements, that is earth, air, fire, water; or the Earth: sky, sea, mountains, valleys, rivers, lakes) to get out of their sight. *Quítensenos* is an instruction to *todos los que no son aptos* to get out of their sight (the pronoun *nos* conveys the sense of 'from us'). The people's eyes are in any case *maravillados*, wonderstruck by the hero.

**Paragraph 4:** She speaks here, in the plural, on behalf of the people. They are moved by a telluric (*telúrica*, meaning belonging to or of the earth) drunkenness (*embriaguez*) on finding that this son they have produced is also God, *hallamos hijo nuestro al mismo Dios*. This is because the Hero, *el Héroe,* is God's essence (*su esencia*) and his science (*su ciencia*). The *su* here and subsequently refers to God. In that case, the speaker also posits that it does not matter if the actions of the Hero, since he is the son, science and essence of God,  are in her favour or against her. If she is to be killed by a hero (a cyclone (*ciclón*), a paroxysm of rage or passion (*arrebato*), a volcano, an ocean), then it does not matter whose side he is on.

114

**Paragraph 5:** In this very brief paragraph, she expresses her wish to die with God, however her death comes (*vengame como me venga*). Her intimation, in the previous paragraph, (*que su heroísmo sea contra mí o a favor mío*) that there is a possibility that the hero may, in fact, be on the side of the enemy allows in a rare but very human scintilla of doubt. Indeed, however disgusted she may have been by the overt political role played by the Church in the conflict, this would not render her entirely immune from the occasional, shattering moment of weakness, however fleeting, in which she may have feared that perhaps the Church was somehow in the right after all, and that God really was on the side of the fascist enemy.

**Paragraph 6:** The perspective shifts in this paragraph back towards a discussion of the admirable nature of the hero, more consonant with the exaltation of the *Übermensch* of fascist ideology but also utterly in keeping with the fashion, on both sides of the propaganda divide, to exalt heroic figures. There was, understandably, a greater tendency on the fascist side, particularly early on, to claim as their own the heroic figures, real and mythological, associated with the Christian reconquest of Spain and the Spanish conquest and colonisation of Latin America while, in poetry on the Republican side, there was a greater emphasis, again understandably, on the heroism of the ordinary, usually unnamed, soldier. Here, the speaker wishes to distance herself from the weak (*débiles*), in the sense of those lacking courage (*cobardes*), even if they are brothers. She prefers to associate herself with the hero, enemy or not, and the good fortune to be had at his hands (*buena suerte la que den sus manos*), implying, one must assume, that death at the hands of such a hero is preferable to a life among cowards.

**Paragraph 7:** In this final paragraph, she raises herself to the level of the hero. In a return to the Greco-Roman world, she says she will take her grievance against the hero, if she is in the right (*si tengo la razón contra él*) and he defeats her (*y él me vence*), to *los dioses*, the gods. In Greco-Roman mythology disputes between the gods and sometimes between heroes and gods were taken to the seat of Zeus on Mount Olympus for arbitration. In the last line, she reiterates her intention of, if necessary, dying for the hero, no matter what side he is on.

115

# Poem XXXII

Caerá el agua siempre, inextinguible, juntando las tierras donde pace hoy anchamente el Duelo. El Agua no se terminará; saldrá de sí eterna como el tiempo en acto. Pura. Presencia infinita del infinito Dios ausente.

Los que sufren vendrán al corro de las aguas caedoras sin límite, con sus sedes resecas y restallantes; sus bocas de pergamino crujidor, víctimas del Llanto que las fue sorbiendo hasta la agonía.

Llueve sobre los pueblos que la Muerte amamanta. Llueve, y suben de nivel los ojos que miran la lluvia. Los enterrados se mecen entre lodos blandísimos, empapados del agua eterna, sin fin.

## Commentary

In the autograph manuscript, this is dated '1939, Valencia' and is the final poem of the *Mientras los hombres mueren* sequence.

**Paragraph 1:** This poem anticipates peace. Water will provide the antidote to the dryness which has pervaded the landscape throughout the sequence, the *suelo seco de luz* of Poem XXIV on which the people's feet can be heard crunching. Lands which are grazed (*pacer* as in animals grazing in a field) by *el Duelo* will be united by the flow of water. The water will emerge from itself (*salir de sí*) as if it were time happening in the very instant in which it exists (*el tiempo en acto*). For the speaker, this water, which is pure, will constitute the infinite presence of an absent infinite God. By definition, God has been absent from the field of battle and the cities under bombardment. This allusion is the first hint of a return.

**Paragraph 2:** Those who suffer will come to *el corro*, a place which is circular in shape, where the waters fall without limit (*las aguas caedoras*). These people, whose thirsts (*sedes*) have been dried up (*resecas*) and *restallantes* (cracked), as in the cracked or parched lips and tongues which go with extreme thirst, have mouths which are like crackling parchment

116

(*pergamino crujidor*). This echoes the use of *crujir* in Poem XXIV to describe a landscape: *los pies que crujían las rebanadas del suelo seco de luz*. The people have been dessicated by grieving, personified as *el Llanto*; the constant weeping has sucked (*sorber*) them dry of all their moisture to the very point of agony (*hasta la agonía*).

**Paragraph 3:** The *pueblos* (towns, villages, communities) which have been suckled (*amamantar*) by *la Muerte* are now experiencing rain. The people are finally able to lift up their eyes (*suben de nivel los ojos*) to look at the rain, a blessing at last from skies that have spewed down bombs on them for so long. Even the dead (*los enterrados*, the buried) benefit, as they rock themselves (*mecerse*) in the very soft mud (*lodos blandísimos*) now soaked (*empapados*) by the eternal rain (*agua eterna, sin fin*).

117

# Poem XXXIII

Ahora que los Hombres han depuesto las armas, ahora que se llaman hermanos y que los vencedores empiezan a hablar de perdón y de olvido, ¿qué piensas tú, Madre?

Madre, que vas de negro, allá y acá de la Patria, ¿qué sientes tú en tu cuerpo de cuna, en tus pechos secos y quemados de arrasante angustia?

Madre de los Muertos, de los Asesinados, de los Fugitivos, qué dices Tú?...

## Commentary

This poem is not included in Conde's autograph manuscript.

**Paragraph 1:** *Madre* (and *Tú*, below in the last paragraph), are in block capitals in Emilio Miró's *Obra poética* (1967). They have an initial capital, as reproduced here, in his *Poesía completa* (2007). The *tú* at the end of the first sentence/question is not capitalised in either edition. This may well be the reason a decision was taken to omit the use of block capitals in the 2007 edition. The important distinction to be made here, irrespective of typographical consistency, is that it is the speaker who is addressing a generic mother figure, not, as is probable, for example, in Poem XXV, Conde addressing her own mother. This generic mother figure represents all the mothers in the sequence who have lost sons. She also probably represents the nation in the sense of *Madre Patria*.

**Paragraph 2:** This second question likens the mother's body to a cradle (*cuerpo de cuna*), first for the unborn child within her and then as she cradles the newborn in her arms. This mother's breasts are dried up and burnt by a devastating (*arrasante*) agony, even as *los Hombres*, and the initial capital here is most likely ironic, walk around speaking blithely of *perdón y olvido*.

**Paragraph 3:** In this final question, she lists a series of avocations of the mother figure, much in the way a litany addressed to the Blessed Virgin would invoke the mother of God. The Litany of Loreto, the oldest and best known litany of the Virgin, approved by Pope Sixtus V in 1587, addresses the Virgin, for example, as: Mother of Christ, Mother of divine grace, Mother most pure, Mother most chaste, Mother inviolate, Mother undefiled and so on. Here, the sequence *Madre de los Muertos, de los Asesinados, de los Fugitivos* performs a similar function and makes definite the association of the mother figure with the Blessed Virgin. In contrast also to the *Hombres* now contemplating *perdón y olvido*, she is the mother of the men who will not make up the apparent post-war consensus. The *Muertos* may be taken as those killed openly in battle or in bombardments and bombing raids and other mass attacks on the civilian population, the *Asesinados* as those killed by stealth or in reprisals. Each of these belongs, to some extent, to both sides. However, the *Fugitivos* can only come from the ranks of the defeated, consisting of the former members of the Republican army or supporters of the government who have been forced into hiding or to flee the country.

# La guerra en el puerto

Broncos, resecos, rítmicos, acompasados: obreros del puerto, descargadores impávidos de afilados navíos huidos, perseguidos, que deshacen los aviones crujidores, explosivos, burlando las dianas de espejos y la vigilia de cañones fieles.

Obreros del puerto, del que no quedan ya piedras blancas ni casas levantadas sobre sus pies de olorosas algas; los que acuden a descargar trigo, azúcar, café, lanas y cartas de ausentes, y alas para los exaltados del vuelo heroico, velas para las barcas de pesca humilde, ruedas para los carros veloces, esencia para los motores tiránicos... ¡Qué hombría tan inhumana, tan sobrehumana la vuestra!

Obreros que entre sirenas nunca de cánticos ni de músicas, hacéis el duelo en vuestras casas por defendernos del hambre; descargadores de imprescindibles riquezas condenadas al fuego, ¡qué arrogancia sin par y sin historia la vuestra!

La ciudad discurre por sus alamedas de frutos, por sus lienzos de verdor, a la esbeltez señora de sus torres alígeras; y el mar brama, resuella, atrae muerte, zumba, lanza sobre el puerto, donde los hombres mueven sus brazos con el peso que trajo el mar... ¡Heroísmo de los sufrimientos, de los que caen tras los que cayeron, antes de los que caerán con sus piramidales caballos normandos y sus carros fuertes, entre hierros negros, con el salor entre los ojos y labios, como un postrer bautismo.

¿Qué hombre de la ciudad, si asustadizo, no se avergüenza frente a estos obreros del puerto? Día a día, enhiestos, atraviesan el duelo de rocas y de jarcias; día a día caen y recaen entre fardos; y las calles marineras se llenan de la sangre que levantaba toneladas, de los dientes que trituraban coraje, de los dedos que cogieron al miedo por el cuello, obligándole a resollar vencido.

Mechones dislocados, ojos azules, frentes a las que el vigor puso huesos indestructibles; y el arranque, el empuje, la varonía sin límites, el ser físico rebosante de voluntad ciclópea frente a los barcos, propicias víctimas todos de la aviación que muerde, retuerce a los hombres, sin llanto ni gemido;

que no caen sobre heces cuando prorrumpe la muerte.

¿Quiénes son los más rudos hombres de lucha, de trabajo, que los descargadores de barcos, infaliblemente bombardeados?

¡Hágase, si se puede, más grande la mar! ¡Hínchase la mar, reálcense los veleros y los bergantines para llegar a este puerto!

Estos colosos requieren estatua de pórfido en el torreón de un mar libre.

## Commentary

Conde read this poem out to an audience of dockers and other port-workers (*los obreros del Grau*) at El Grau on 15 December 1938. It is dated 28 November 1938 on her manuscript. El Grau, now a *barrio* of Valencia, was one of several coastal *pueblos*, known in Valencian as the *Poblats Marítims*, incorporated into the port of Valencia in 1897 when the city underwent major urban expansion. It is the only poem in the collection which she is known to have read in front of an audience and is, perhaps, as a consequence, much less introspective and abstract than many of the other poems in the sequence. She addresses the dockers, describing their activities and the importance of these activities to the survival of the city and lauds their heroism. This poem is not included in the manuscript original sequence for *Mientras los hombres mueren*.

**Paragraph 1:** Conde opens with a series of adjectives describing the dockers as they unload (*descargar*) cargo (*broncos*, gruff, *resecos*, dry or hardened, *acompasados*, measured, moving to a beat (*compás*) in the sense of the natural rhythms of the unloading process, echoing the use of *rítmicos*). They are also undaunted or impassive (*impávidos*) in spite of the constant dangers they must run. Meanwhile, the ships they unload nip in and out as swiftly as possible, ready to flee at a moment's notice (*huidos*, the sense of fleeing danger, *afilados*, the sense of sharp watchfulness). The bomber aircraft, the third player in this drama, make crunching noises (*crujidores*), the noises of engines, machine-guns, explosions. They are *explosivos*, avoiding (*burlando*) the traps laid for them by decoy mirrors (*dianas de espejos*; *diana*, a bull's-eye or target) set to reflect sunlight and confuse the pilots. The ack-ack fire (*la vigilia,* the vigilance) of the anti-aircraft guns in the port (*cañones fieles*) seems to have little effect against the bombers. It is interesting that, even at this late stage, she should use the adjective *fieles* to describe the anti-aircraft guns, a branch of the military still loyal to the elected government. This is possibly because Valencia was bombarded by Nationalist warships as well as by German Condor Legion and Italian Legionary Airforce bombers based in Mallorca. Here, she appears to be exclusively referring to aerial bombardment.

**Paragraph 2:** In this paragraph, she points to the destruction already visited on El Grau. There are no buildings left standing on the seafront or, as she puts it, on their feet of sweetly-smelling algae (*pies de olorosas algas*). She then lists the commodities unloaded by the dockers: everyday foodstuffs such as sugar, coffee and *trigo* (wheat or grain); *lanas* (wool) and letters from the absent. Those absent might be adults already in exile or even the children of Republican families sent to friendly countries for their own safety for the duration of the war. She also cites materials necessary for modern warfare: *alas para los exaltados del vuelo heroico*, wings (*alas*) which might mean wings or spare parts for planes, for the air force, those exalted by heroic flight. The Spanish air force, minuscule by comparison with the major Western European powers before the war, had been incorporated early on into the Nationalist camp. Thus, while Spanish biplanes (*Chatos*) were manufactured in Reus-Sabadell for the Republic during the war, the Republican government was heavily dependent, from the outset, on Soviet-supplied planes and pilots. Indeed, so bereft were the Republican military of flight personnel that Spanish pilots initially had to be trained in Russia. The first of these returned to begin active service in September 1937, well over a year after the outbreak of hostilities. The other vital components the dockers unload consist of sails (*velas*) for humble fishing boats, tyres (*ruedas*) for cars or even armoured vehicles (*carros veloces*) and, of course, fuel (*esencia*) for the tyrannical engines (*motores tiránicos*) of these vehicles. In all, the dockers display a manliness (*hombría*) which is both inhuman and superhuman in its ability to achieve the impossible.

**Paragraph 3:** In this third paragraph, she continues to address the dockers directly (*Obreros que entre sirenas*). They work amid air-raid sirens (*sirenas*) which she compares to the sirens of literature and music (*nunca de cánticos ni de músicas*) who represent a different kind of danger, being the alluring female figures of mythology who entice men to their deaths in deep rivers with their beautiful song. Here, *cánticos* may indicate songs in the sense of canticles or chants, these being mostly religious while *músicas* probably refers more to secular music. These dockers are obliged to bring grief and mourning to their own houses (*hacéis el duelo en vuestras casas*) because there are inevitable casualties as they put their lives at risk in order to defend the people of the city (*defendernos*) from hunger. The items they unload, however mundane or technical they may seem when listed separately, constitute, of course, indispensable riches (*imprescindibles riquezas*) to the people of a dwindling territory under siege. *Condenadas al fuego* indicates that the goods are as much under fire as the men handling them. The attritional, trench warfare-style Battle of the Ebro, which the Nationalists won decisively, ended on 16 November 1938, after which the army of the Republic was no longer a functional fighting force. In December 1938, the Battle for Barcelona would begin. The city would fall on 26 January 1939 and the government of the Republic would go into exile in France on 5 February. In the interim, the dockers going about their business under fire, conduct themselves with unrivalled (*sin par*) arrogance never before seen in history (*sin historia*). The direct eulogy addressed to the dockers ends here and she moves on to deal in more detail with conditions in the city.

**Paragraph 4:** In the first sentence, Conde contrasts the city and the port. In the city, life is going on (*discurrir*) along avenues lined with fruit (*alamedas de frutos*, fruit picked and sold in markets or the produce hanging on fruit trees). Some of the city presents canvasses of greenery (*lienzos de verdor*), presumably the green parks and trees in the city. In this panorama, the old city would be most clearly identified by the seigneurial or noble slenderness (*la esbeltez señora*) of its winged towers (*las torres aligeras*). The *Torres de Serranos* and the *Torres de Quart* are sets of medieval twin towers which form two of the best-preserved and most well-known gates in the old city walls. In contrast, the sea roars (*bramar*), breathes heavily (*resollar*), attracts death, hums (*zumbar*), casts itself (*lanzar*) onto the port where the men are busy unloading the cargo (*el peso*, weight) which came from the sea. The caesura which ends this sentence allows time to develop the contrast. Then she moves on to extol the heroism of the fallen, past, present and future. They fall as they work with their cart horses (*piramidales caballos normandos*). These Norman (*normandos*) horses are probably the descendants of medieval warhorses. The Norman or Anglo-Norman horse was used by the Normans from the Middle Ages. These were large and powerful animals, usually over 16 hands high, perfectly suited to work as carthorses in civilian society. The word *piramidales* may describe the strength and physical solidity of these

123

animals, or it may allude to the shape of the caparison (a large cape), often reinforced with armour plating and chainmail or placed over an undercoat of these two materials, which could, in medieval times, cover the horse from neck to tail and fall almost to the hooves. Equally, *los carros fuertes*, in actuality, the carts these horses are harnessed to, may allude to the war chariots of Roman times. Here, man, beast and cart must brave dark metal (*hierros negros*, either shrapnel or bomb-ravaged metal) and brine (*salor*) in a last baptism (*un postrer bautismo*).

**Paragraph 5:** In this paragraph, she draws a comparison between the ordinary men of the city (*¿qué hombre de la ciudad?*) and the dockers. Her rhetorical question suggests that even the most timorous of male citizens (*si asustadizo*) should be shamed by these dockers. These men who hold themselves so upright (*enhiestos*) must make their way through rocks and ship's rigging (*jarcias*). This way is a *via dolorosa*, a way of suffering for them (*el duelo de rocas y de jarcias*) because it will bring them death and dismemberment. They will fall among the bales (*fardos*, i.e. the merchandise and equipment they carry) and their blood will fill the *calles marineras* (the streets of the sea): the sea itself or the docks. In a sequence of three, she lists: this blood which once carried loads (*que levantaba toneladas*, tonnes), the teeth which chewed (*triturar*) on courage, the fingers which took fear by the scruff of the neck (*coger por el cuello*) and made it pant with breathlessness in defeat (*resollar vencido*).

**Paragraph 6:** She returns, in this paragraph, to her description of the dockers. This time, her language is more abstract, as she enumerates the physical traits which constitute their strength. Their tousled hair (*mechones dislocados*), their blue eyes (blue probably because it reflects the sea, rather than because it is the common eye colour of these men), their foreheads (*frentes*) in which vigour (*vigor*) placed indestructible bones (*huesos*), all indicate heroic stature. Their strength is conveyed in the terms *arranque* (a fit of rage or passion, or the energy which starts something off), *empuje*, (initial force or impulse) and *varonía* (manliness); these qualities are limitless (*sin límites*). Together they form a physical being brimming over (*rebosante*) with a force of will (*voluntad*) which is *ciclópea*, Cyclopean. This refers to *Cíclope*, Cyclops, a one-eyed giant in Greek mythology, one of a group of Cyclopes. Among other feats, they were often credited with the construction of ancient city walls. In spite of this inhuman power, the dockers nonetheless become the opportune (*propicias*) victims of the bombers. Indeed, the bomber aircraft are themselves like mythological beasts in that they bite (*aviación que muerde*) and twist the men's bodies. This is an evocation of the primeval battles between heroes and monsters in Greek and other mythologies. The men fall bravely, that is, *sin llanto ni gemido*. Lastly, they are so courageous that they will not fall on excrement (*heces*) when their hour of death comes (*cuando prorrumpe la muerte*). Their end will be dignified.

**Paragraph 7:** She returns in this paragraph to a more recognisably direct form of address. Her rhetorical question asks if there are any tougher men (*los más rudos hombres*) than the dockers, infallibly (*infaliblemente*, meaning that the bombing is unerring in its accuracy) bombed.

**Paragraph 8:** Here she calls for the sea to be made grander to accommodate these giants of men. *Hínchase la mar* (let the sea swell) follows on from *hágase más grande la mar* and she uses the more poetic, *la mar*. The sailing ships (*veleros*) and brigantines (*bergantines*, a type of large sailing ship used as a merchant vessel, and most famously associated with piracy) should rise up and become beautiful once more (*realzarse*) on such an enlarged sea. This is, no doubt, an allusion to the greatness of the Spanish sailing fleet in previous centuries and the importance of Valencia as a major Mediterranean port. By the 1930s, most major seafaring trade was conducted in fossil-fuel freighters which did not even have sails, though there would certainly have been much use of sail power and smaller boats for local transit during the war due to fuel shortages.

**Paragraph 9:** This last paragraph pays a final, consummate tribute to the dockers. They are like giants (*colosos*), so they need a grand sea populated with great ships as a backdrop. The Colossus of Rhodes was one of the wonders of the ancient world, a huge statue of the god Helios which stood at the entrance of the harbour at Rhodes. It was destroyed in an earthquake in 224 BC, just 66 years after its construction. Here Conde demands that a statue made of porphyry (a purplish stone, a bit like marble, used since ancient Greek times to denote royalty and honour), be erected in honour of the dockers. It should be placed on a large tower (*torreón,* usually part of a castle wall or built in a town square for defensive purposes). Here, because the sea is referred to in a more factual way, it is *un mar*.

It is worth noting that this long poem is very carefully paced in terms of its accessibility, given that it was read aloud in public at least once and to an audience defined by occupation and domicile, not interest in culture. Paragraphs 1–3 are highly repetitive and rhetorical, using lists (of nouns or adjectives) and exclamations, and describing the daily reality of the dockers' lives in language which does not stray too far into the abstract or the obscure. In Paragraphs 4–6, which are relatively longer than the others, Conde employs more complex imagery and uses a wider lexical and referential range. It is unlikely that an audience of dockers and others employed in the port of El Grau would have found them easy to understand. However, she moves, in the final three paragraphs, to remedy any loss of orientation in her general audience and closes with a sequence of three short paragraphs eulogising the dockers in straightforward and highly emotive terms, incorporating imagery and classical/historical reference which would be recognisable to all.

# Era una palabra

Ya está muerta, ya consumida; virgen desflorada, doncella estrujada y fatigada por la tumba de la posesión inconsciente.

No la veréis, porque acaba de huir ante mis sienes, llena de fango de su muerte. En vano gritaremos su nombre trivalente; su inicial líquida, su puente como beso rotundo, su claro final seco, estampido del tumulto.

Ya no la veréis, hombres que corristeis tras sus sonrisa. Ya no la veréis, mujeres que bajo su mirada os sentisteis salvar.

¿Existió un día entre la confusa muchedumbre de clamores, de risas, de saltos y de asaltos? ¿Fue posible su relámpago pineal cuando yacían los negros caballos de la rutina o el desenfreno?...

¡Si fuistéis a por ella, a horadar montañas de cemento que la apartaban!, ¿qué hicistéis con su hermosura maltratada? ¿Qué gesto, cuál brutal palabra, qué mentira grasienta y blanducha espantó su figura ágil, espesándola, hundiéndola, envejeciéndola hasta la agonía?...

¡Ay hombres que sucumbisteis y hombres que prevalecieron!... ¿Qué hicisteis todos de la Libertad?

## Commentary

This poem is not included in Conde's autograph manuscript. It is in the form of an extended riddle, where several definitions of a mystery word are provided, and the word itself is not identified until the end.

**Paragraph 1:** Consumed (*consumida*) is used as a synonym for death in the sense of being used up. This word, as yet unidentified, is a deflowered virgin (*virgen desflorada*). Virginity is synonymous with purity; here this purity has been interfered with. To continue the metaphor, the maiden (*doncella*) has been squeezed dry (*estrujada*) and worn out (*fatigada*). Furthermore, the act of possession, which took her virginity/purity, has been an unconscious act (*la posesión inconsciente*) that has led to her incarceration in a tomb. In sum, this is an outrage brought about

127

by complacency. Indeed, the figure of Liberty (*Libertad*) is usually represented as a beautiful woman, consistent with the invocation of *virgen* and *doncella* in this opening paragraph. In Roman times, statues were erected to the goddess *Libertas*, the goddess of freedom. In modern times, the US Statue of Liberty, for example, or the French Revolutionary figure, *Marianne*, embody this ideal.

**Paragraph 2:** At this stage, Liberty has fled, as the speaker was watching (*sienes*, the temples on the sides of the head). She will now be covered in mud (*fango*), the mud of her own death, her purity besmirched. The second sentence analyses the syllabic structure of the word. It is trivalent (*trivalente*, made up of three syllables), it has a liquid first syllable (*su inicial líquido*, the liquid beginning, *Li-*); a bridge (*su puente*, middle syllable) like a round kiss (*como beso rotundo*, *-ber-*, similar to *bes-* in *beso* or *besar*) and a clearcut final syllable (*su claro final seco*, *-tad*) which is like the bang or report (*estampido*) of a tumult or crowd.

**Paragraph 3:** The speaker addresses women and men separately in this paragraph, explaining that they will not see this figure anymore, not the men who ran after her smile, not the women who felt themselves to be saved beneath her gaze.

**Paragraph 4:** From the perspective of imminent or actual defeat, the speaker now asks if indeed Liberty ever existed. *¿Existió un día?* has a sense of 'did it ever exist?' in a climate of noise and shouting (*clamores*), laughter, *saltos y asaltos* (leaps, perhaps of faith, and assaults). Then she offers a contrast between routine (*la rutina*) and its opposite, headlong permissiveness (*el desenfreno*), which seem to be the twin faces of struggle, and wonders if Liberty could have existed amid either of these. Both are here depicted as black horses (*los caballos negros*) lying dead (*yacían*), an indication that war kills whether its victims are at that moment conforming to a routine or engaged in unrestricted or lawless activity. *Pineal* relates to the pineal gland in the brain which regulates melatonin and sleep patterns. Though there is an apparent contradiction between lightning (*relámpago*) on the one hand and a gland which regulates sleep on the other, this may be an allusion to the way in which Liberty may itself be a manifestation of power properly controlled, regulated lightning, as it were. Her question remains as to whether Liberty existed under these conditions, anticipating a future, perhaps, in which the war will be remembered, erroneously, as a golden age of Liberty.

**Paragraph 5:** In this paragraph, the speaker interrogates those who sought for Liberty in an overt way. They were prepared to drill through (*horadar*) mountains of cement to get to her. These mountains of cement might represent public buildings or prisons, entities which kept Liberty apart (*apartar*) from the people. When they found her in her condition of mistreated beauty (*su hermosura maltratada*), echoing the opening image of a *virgen desflorada, doncella estrujada y fatigada*, these seekers after Liberty appear also to have traduced her. This may be an indictment of politicians and activists alike. She asks what (*cuál*, in the sense of *qué*) greasy (*grasienta*), flabby (*blanducha*) lie they used to frighten (*espantar*) the agile young figure of this beautiful goddess (*figura ágil*) so that it thickened (*espesar*), sank (*hundir*) and aged to the point of agony.

**Paragraph 6:** She concludes with a ringing condemnation of politicians and activists in this paragraph. On both sides, Liberty was betrayed. These *hombres*, those who succumbed (*sucumbir*) and those who prevailed (*prevalecer*), are not to be confused with the generality of the dead and the dying whose agony she accompanies and to which she gives voice in the poetry of *Mientras los hombres mueren*. She draws a marked line here between those ordinary men who died because they had no choice and those, on both sides, who orchestrated the conflict.

# Ha terminado la guerra

Han aullado los barcos, y en los sombríos muelles las torrenciales agonías de millares de hombres que querían huir, vencidos.

Los audaces alcanzaron nave que los salvara. Pero ¡cuántos andan llorando su derrota y caminan con sed y con hambre! Sin monedas, sin mano amiga que les otorgue consuelo...

Como un súbito alud inmensísimo terminó la guerra.

Se desplomó la paz.

## Commentary

The original version in Conde's autograph manuscript is longer and more explicit. See Appendix 2. It is not part of the manuscript sequence for *Mientras los hombres mueren*.

**Paragraph 1:** She deploys the verb *aullar*, to howl, to indicate the sound of ships' horns as they prepare to depart. This verb reflects the enormous agony of grief and waiting (*torrenciales agonías*) endured by soldiers and other supporters of the Republic as they crowd on the docks (*muelles*) desperate to board the last ships leaving Valencia before the city falls completely under Nationalist rule.

**Paragraph 2:** Only the audacious (*los audaces*) manage to save themselves. The rest, the majority, must endure the sorrow of defeat, thirst and hunger. Refugees in their own land, there is no-one to assist them, they have no money.

**Paragraph 3:** Thus, the war finally comes to an end, and she describes it as a sudden and immense landslide (*alud*, a landslide or an avalanche). It is so because the end of the war does not mean peace with liberty for Valencia, it means enemy invasion.

**Paragraph 4:** Therefore, the advent of peace is more like a collapse or a plunge (*desplomarse*). Since she has already invoked *alud*, this must be a plunge down into an abyss.

# A los niños muertos por la guerra

## Poem I

¡No los deshojéis, cañones; no los tricéis, ametralladoras; bombas grandísimas que caéis del cielo hondo y que parecéis dones de las nubes anchas, no rompáis los cuerpecitos de los niños!

¿No siente el plomo piedad de estos hombros de leche rosada, de estas sangrecitas dulces, de estas pieles de labios? ¿Ningún aviador enemigo tiene niñitos que levanten sus manos al viento de las hélices?

No. El enemigo no parece padre, y acaso es huérfano también. Por eso los niños se quiebran en tajos humeantes, y hay por los jardines cabelleras de musgos, rodillas con seda rasgada; suelto todo entre los árboles quebrados, con duelo sostenido de gritos que ayer eran cometas y hoy son pobres encías partidas que ya no gustarán mazorcas ni pezones frescos de madres enamoradas...

### Commentary

The original title in the autograph manuscript is 'Poemas a los niños muertos en la guerra'. See commentary on Conde's preface to this collection. I have followed Miró.

**Paragraph 1:** The speaker addresses the instruments of war: the cannon (*cañones*), the machine-guns (*ametralladoras*), the bombs, and begs them not to tear apart the little bodies (*los cuerpecitos*) of the children. Time and time again, when referring to children she will use diminutives (*cuerpo – cuerpecito*) as is the Spanish custom when dealing with the attributes and activities of children. To a child's eye, the bombs falling from the sky might appear to be gifts falling from heaven (*dones de las nubes anchas*). This interest in representing the realities of war from a child's perspective is a constant of this sequence of poems.

**Paragraph 2:** *El plomo* (lead) is a reference to the metal content in bombs and bullets, which would not necessarily be lead, though lead is the metal most widely associated by the general public with shot. The children's shoulders are likened to milk (*leche rosada*), their blood is mentioned in diminutive (*sangrecitas dulces*) as are the children themselves in the next sentence (*niñitos*). Their skins are *pieles de labios,* skin which is so soft it feels as if it is made entirely of lips. In the second sentence she relates, for the first time, the family life of enemy aircrew (*ningún aviador enemigo*) to the lives of the children on the ground they are bombing. All aircraft were powered by propellers (*hélices*) in the 1930s. Children could be fascinated by the wind produced by propellers, and would be inclined, in the first instance, to see a warplane as a thing of wonder. The speaker asks if this is not also true of the enemy pilot's children who would have no reason to associate their father's occupation with war.

Paragraph 3: She concludes in the first sentence that the enemy must be both childless and parentless. This is the only explanation she can find for the bombing of children. Thus, the fragments of children, broken up (*quebrarse*) in steaming bomb craters (*tajos*, slashes, *humeantes*), and the gardens in which children would normally have played contain hair covered in moss (*cabelleras de musgos*) and knees, probably dismembered, still covered in torn silk (*rodillas con seda rasgada*). All this is scattered (*suelto todo*) among the trees in the same gardens which are also shattered. The cries (of the dying children) which now make up a sustained sorrow (*duelo sostenido*) were once, before the bombing, like comets (*cometas*), bringing hope, since a comet may be a harbinger of good tidings; or kites flown by the children in better times. Now, though, there are only the split gums (*encías partidas*) which will never again taste or enjoy (*gustarán*) corn cobs (*mazorcas*) or the milk from their mothers' nipples (*pezones*). Corn cobs were given to children to suck on when they were teething or if they were hungry. The caesura, at the end, opens up the image.

# Poem II

Las verdes caracolas del espanto, y los atronadores murmullos del terror, y el viscoso largo-azul dedo del miedo... ¡Corred, niños, corred por los caminos limpios de pólvora, sin cerebros machacados todavía, hacia las aguas tranquilas, serenas, del silencio y de la vida!

¡Corred, chiquillos a los que buscan las púas de las ametralladoras! ¡Dejad atrás a los hombres, desoíd a las mujeres, no escuchéis otra voz que la del viento, la de las bestias sanas y vitales; la voz de la continuidad cósmica, desbaratándose a vuestras espaldas, pero en sí permanente más allá del morir!

Aquí, la muerte; aquí, lo negro; aquí, la guerra... ¡Corred, niños, corred con el mañana!

## Commentary

**Paragraph 1:** The speaker warns the children to run away from danger. This is the same nightmarish world she describes from the perspective of adults in *Mientras los hombres mueren*, but now from a child's-eye view. The green conch shells (*caracolas*) of horror/shock/fright (*del espanto*), the thundering (*atronadores*), the rumblings of terror (*murmullos del terror*) and the viscous (*viscoso*) long, blue (*largo-azul*) finger of fear are all images from a child's nightmare where shape, texture, sound and colour assume grotesque proportions, and fear and horror come more directly clothed in organic form and colour than would be the case with adults. The green and blue might well be the (greenish grey) planes in the (blue) sky, and the noise they make that of thunder. The speaker allows a caesura for the images to develop, and then moves on to order the children to run away. They should run along paths not yet covered in the debris from bombs and shells (*limpios de pólvora*, gunpowder), not yet paved with crushed skulls (*cerebros machacados*). This is the nightmare which awaits them if they stay. She urges them towards a lost and therefore inaccessible paradise, a lost pastoral scene of *aguas tranquilas, serenas*, a place where there is silence and life.

**Paragraph 2:** She repeats her injunction to the children, here using the diminutive *chiquillos*. They should run away because they are being sought out (*a los que buscan*) by the hedgehog spines or quills (*púas*) spewed out by machine-guns. Again, she employs a nature image which would appeal to a child's imagination, perhaps even to make the piercing of the bullets more real to a child. They should therefore not heed adults, men or women (*desoír*, deliberately not to listen to) and place their trust in nature, in *el viento*, in *las bestias sanas y vitales* (healthy and alive). The world of adults, has, after all, let them down. Behind their backs, the voice of cosmic continuity (*la continuidad cósmica*) is falling into ruin and destruction (*desbaratándose*), yet it is the one thing which will also survive (*en sí permanente más allá del morir*). This implies that there will be a future for the children as long as they can escape the destruction of the present.

**Paragraph 3:** She makes the contrast between present and future clear in this last sentence. In the world of adults (*aquí*) there is only blackness (*lo negro*) and war. Beyond that, beyond the caesura, the children must run, towards or with the future (*el mañana*, tomorrow as in the future, as opposed to *la mañana*, tomorrow as in the next morning).

# Poem III

¡Que no griten las sirenas sobre las trémulas orejitas de las campanas de oro!

¡Que se quiebran todas las alas que rajan el curvo cielo de las noches cóncavas!

¡Que no rematen en bocas negras los cilindros por donde se derrama el odio!

¿Es que todos olvidaron las cunas, las cunas donde ríen solos y solos cantan los niños?...

## Commentary

Three injunctions are followed by a rhetorical question here. The children's ears, in diminutive (*orejitas*) and tremulous (*trémulas*), are likened to golden bells (*campanas de oro*) which must not be disturbed by the noise of air-raid sirens (*sirenas*). These images point up the contrast between the idyllic (*campanas de oro*) and the awful reality of *sirenas* which, as in 'La guerra en el puerto', have nothing to do with music. She would like to see all those wings, meaning aircraft, which tear up (*rajar*) the night sky to be shattered. The sky is curved (*curvo*) and the nights concave (*cóncavas*). This has a sense of the Aristotelian notion of a flat earth and a curving firmament above, in which modern war machines are utterly out of place. In the third injunction, bombs and bullets become cylinders out of which hatred spills (*derramarse*). They end up (*rematar en*) as black mouths, perhaps as they explode. The rhetorical question asks then if in all this everyone has forgotten the cradles (*las cunas*). The use of *solos* twice, to describe the children singing and laughing, emphasises their vulnerability in the face of these weapons of destruction.

# Poem IV

Iba el niño por entre los cuatro riachuelos de cuatro esquinas frías. Llevaba en las manos, mojadas de naranja, un caballo de cartón azul...

¿Quién le clavó a la tierra con la espoleta helicoidal de la bomba? ¿De qué ángeles perversos se desgajaron cuchillas de acero?

Quedóse el caballo salvo, tibio de sangre limpia, cabe el aliento de humo del avión... ¡Quién viera la calle doblada de espanto, partirse en cascos de piedra visceral bajo los pedazos de niño explotado!

## Commentary

**Paragraph 1:** This appears to be a narration of a real event. The use of *cuatro*, meaning 'a few', renders the background to this atrocity as general as possible. The *riachuelos* (little streams) might be streams or even water in the gutters of the *cuatro esquinas frías*. Against this, Conde provides two striking details: the little boy's hands were sticky with the juice of oranges (*mojadas de naranja*) and he carried in them a very simple toy, a blue, cardboard horse.

**Paragraph 2:** She asks who nailed him (*clavar*) to the ground with the helix-shaped fuse (*espoleta heliocoidal*) of a bomb. The mention of helicoidal perhaps evokes the enemy aviator's children of Poem I ('Niños') *que levanten sus manos al viento de las hélices* and the resultant contrast. She likens the bombers to *ángeles perversos*. In any child's universe, the skies might well be populated by angels; in an inherently Catholic country, whatever the prevailing political climate, all children would be aware of the role of the guardian angel. Here, however, these are depicted as perverse beings who allow steel knives (*cuchillos de acero*) to be unleashed from their bodies (*desgajarse*).

**Paragraph 3:** Poignantly, the cardboard horse, made of much flimsier stuff than the little boy, is unharmed (*salvo*). *Quedóse* is an archaic (old) usage of *se quedó*, it remained. It is most likely employed here to evoke the style of a *romance*, a traditional ballad, which might have narrated just such an event. The horse, however, though intact, is still covered in the lukewarm (*tibio*) blood of the dead child. This blood is, of course, *sangre limpia*, emphasising the essential innocence of the little boy. In the immediate aftermath, there is a sense of (*caber*, there is room for) the plane; the smell (*el aliento*, the breath) of its exhaust fumes hangs over the scene. *Quién viera* is used in the rhetorical sense of 'who could possibly look at?' as she describes the street bent double in pain and shock, split apart in *cascos de piedra visceral* (in this case *cascos*, usually shells, are shards, of visceral stone) beneath the pieces (*los pedazos*) of the body of the dead child, *el niño explotado*, the child blown to pieces.

# Poem V

Yo dolía por un hijo. Toda mi entraña se abría en sed de un hijo. ¡Ah, que ya sé por qué mi vigilante espíritu no quiso desgajarse una rama!

Pero soy madre crucificada en todos los niños que saltaron en chispas por ímpetu de la ronca metralla enemiga. Y estoy doliendo hasta donde se acaba la sangre de mi vientre.

## Commentary

Since Conde was childless at the time of writing and remained so, it would be easy to read this as an autobiographical poem. However, given the strictures the speaker issues to would-be mothers in *Mientras los hombres mueren*, it might be as well to take into account the role of prophet and leader of her people the speaker has already elected for herself and, in particular, the statement the speaker makes in Poem IX (*Mientras*): *cierto que yo no pariré hijo de carne mientras la Tierra haya las furias amarillas de la Guerra*. The verb which she uses in the previous poem to indicate the bombs dropped by warplanes is employed here in a more positive context, that of a tree budding a new branch (*desgajarse una rama*) and creating new life. Her understanding of her childlessness returns her to the role of prophet and mother of her people. Indeed, she becomes a Christlike figure, a *madre crucificada* (crucified mother), suffering every time a child is blown up (*saltar en chispas*) by enemy bombs (*la metralla enemiga*). This causes her pain which reaches in to where the blood of her womb ends.

# Poem VI

La fruta de tu vientre era un verde racimo que besaba tu madre, que besaba yo con labios nuevos y dulces, abriéndose la risa del gozo con nuestro júbilo de besarte.

Ya estamos las dos paradas ante tu yelo. Que una muerte múltiple, enmarañada de cascotes y de trilita, te ha desgarrado de la vida en que te arbolábamos.

¡Ay, muerto niño en flor de azúcares; ay, chiquillo de sangre desparramada!

## Commentary

This poem, like Poem IV ('Niños'), is almost certainly an account of a real event. Both Conde and the child's mother would kiss *la fruta de tu vientre*, the child's abdomen, presumably when the little boy was a baby, as if it were a green cluster (*verde racimo*), as in a bunch of grapes the *verde* connoting extreme youth. The women found great joy (*júbilo de besarte*) in caressing the baby in this way; it produced *la risa del gozo*, in them or indeed in him. Now, however, they are both looking at his corpse, *yelo* representing the coldness of the body after death. (See commentary on Poem XI (*Mientras*).) He has been the victim of a bombing and has died with others (*una muerte múltiple*), a death tangled up in (*enmarañada*) rubble (*cascotes*) and explosive. *Trilita* (*trinitrolueno*), trinitrotoluene or TNT, is a powerful high explosive. The little boy was thus torn from the life in which these women had raised him up, celebrated him (*en que te arbolábamos*). Thus, he has died in the flower of his sweetness (*en flor de azúcares*). The last line, beginning with *¡Ay!* and addressing the dead boy twice, each time in terms of an attribute denoting the manner of his death, is in the form of conventional lament.

# Poem VII

La tierra está nutriéndose de cuerpecillos débiles, pero crecientes y poderosos de luz, para henchirla mejor que el sol, que tan honda no la calara nunca.

¡Niños, niños da la guerra al polvo seco y áspero, mordido de lirios y de mariposas; niños tiernos del abrazo que se dieron sus padres, bajo la metralla trizados como mazorcas que desgrana una mano de hierro!

La tierra sembrada de generaciones en agraz, ¡qué espléndida cosecha de entrañas dará al futuro, hermanos transidos de la guerra!

## Commentary

**Paragraph 1:** The theme developed in *Mientras los hombres mueren* of the bodies of the (young) battlefield dead becoming part of the earth, in Poem II (*Mientras*), for example, where she declares *la tierra está nutrida de simientes frescas*, is extended here to take in the children killed in bombing raids on cities. This time it is the fragile little bodies of the children which feed the earth (*cuerpecillos débiles*). Like the battlefield dead, which in Poem II (*Mientras*) nourish the land because *devuelven intacto el caudal de generaciones que no tuvieron tiempo de crear*, here the bodies of the children are so powerful with light (*poderosos de luz*) that they will cause the land to expand (*henchir*) better than the sun because the sun can never penetrate it so deeply (*que tan honda no la calara nunca*).

**Paragraph 2:** War gives children to the dry and harsh earth (*polvo seco y áspero*). The earth, as a result, is bitten (*mordido*) by lilies (*lirios*) and butterflies (*mariposas*). The lily has connotations of purity or death, the butterflies allude to beauty but also to the shortness of life; both of these are encapsulated in the dead children. These children, the tender (*tiernos*) fruit of their parents' lovemaking (*el abrazo que se dieron sus padres*) are now smashed to pieces (*trizados*) by the bombs (*metralla*). The image of corn cobs (*mazorcas*) is revisited here, in that the dead children are now

141

likened to corn kernels picked from the cob (*desgranar*), not by children's mouths, as in Poem I ('Niños'), rather by *una mano de hierro*, the iron referring to bombs and bullets.

**Paragraph 3:** Just as in Poem II (*Mientras*), the land is now sown (*sembrada*) with these unripe (*en agraz, agraz* is an unripe grape) generations. The speaker, with no little sarcasm, declares it will bring forth a splendid harvest (*cosecha*) in future, but it will be, grotesquely, a harvest of children's guts (*entrañas*). In this final phrase, she addresses her *hermanos transidos de la guerra*, presumably the adults wracked by the grief caused by the war, by the loss of all these children.

# Poem VIII

Mi hijo vive conmigo, va dentro de mi sangre, pero no os lo daré nunca si antes de que mi cuerpo esté seco no alejáis eternamente la guerra de nuestro suelo.

Yo no me abriré en fruto para que vuestro fruto me dé la muerte.

## Commentary

The speaker, who has recorded her inability to produce a child in Poem V ('Niños'), *mi vigilante espíritu no quiso desgajarse una rama* now suggests that a child does exist within her, in her blood (*va dentro de mi sangre*). She appears to direct herself to those fomenting war, to those who might be her enemies (*no os lo daré nunca*). She will not, however, surrender this child while there is still war in the land, even if this means she becomes infertile and unable to produce this child before the war ends (*antes de que mi cuerpo esté seco*). In the final image, she counterbalances the undescended fruit of her body (*yo no me abriré en fruto*) against the fruit of her enemies (*vuestro fruto*), which might well be their sons who become soldiers or the bombs and bullets they employ in warfare. Either way, she anticipates her own death in this (*para que vuestro fruto me dé la muerte*); one would expect this to be brought about by grief at losing her child.

# Poem IX

¡Que nadie le hable al niño de la muerte dada por mano del hombre!
¿Es posible soñar con el amor, enseñando la mano del que odia?

**Commentary**

This poem is epigrammatic, that is pithy, compact and opaque. It plays
with the image of *la mano*. In the first sentence *la mano* can bring death
to a child or children (*la muerte dada por mano del hombre*). The speaker
insists that no-one should speak to the children killed by the hands of men.
One possible interpretation is that the child, though utterly innocent, is,
in death, sullied by the atrocity committed by the adult who murdered
him. In the second sentence, she asks if it is possible to dream of love
(*soñar con el amor*), while at the same time showing the hand of he who
hates (*el que odia*). Perhaps love cannot even be dreamt of in a situation of
fratricidal conflict, or indeed, war in general.

# Poem X

Mujeres que vais de luto porque el odio os trajo la muerte a vuestro regazo, ¡negaos a concebir hijos mientras los hombres no borren la guerra del mundo!

¡Negaos a parir al hombre que mañana matará al hombre hijo de tu hermana, a la mujer que parirá otro hombre para que mate a tu hermano!

## Commentary

In her most forthright statement to women on the withholding of maternity in wartime, the speaker addresses all child-bearing women, women who are dressed in mourning (*que vais de luto*) for the children they have already lost, because hatred (*el odio*) brought death to their laps (*regazo*), asking them to refuse to conceive any further children until men erase (*mientras los hombres no borren*) war from the world. *Mientras los hombres no borren la guerra* provides, of course, an inevitable echo of the title of the collection, *mientras los hombres mueren*. The implication is that while men are dying in war, it is also their creation. This is underlined in the second sentence which establishes a murderous symmetry between the women who give birth to men who kill and the women whose sons are killed by them. Male children will go on to kill, female children to produce male killers.

# Poem XI

¡Si las madres alzaran a sus hijos como teas de alegría! ¡Si las que llevan hijos dentro señalaran sus vientres donde sangres felices se mueven! ¡Si las mujeres oyeran el clamor de sus entrañas, acabarían las guerras!

Porque todos los hombres que caen muertos, y las mujeres que acribilla la metralla, ¡han dado su hijo, que llora y sangra en la guerra!

## Commentary

This poem had a final line which is crossed out in Conde's autograph manuscript: 'sin otra razón para sufrir que el odio de los padres de sus compañeros los niños todos que duelen llanto!' The premise the speaker puts forward here seems to be an impossible one. Her first image, if only women who had children would hold them up like torches of joy (*teas de alegría*) has inevitable echoes of the infinitely darker use of *tea* in *Mientras los hombres mueren*: in Poem I (*Mientras*) she speaks of a *día de espanto abrasado por teas de gritos*; in Poem XVIII, *teas de muertos verdes de vida*. Her second exhortation, if only pregnant women would point to their wombs *donde sangres felices se mueven*, goes counter to her previous injunction to women, in Poem X ('Niños') that they should refuse to conceive while the war lasts. Her last, if only women listened to their wombs (*el clamor de sus entrañas*) *acabarían las guerras!* is so blatantly impossible an aspiration that it becomes clear that this entire paragraph does not proffer a solution to war, rather it points up the endless sacrifice of children. The final sentence drives home the intensity of loss experienced by everyone, male and female. Both the men who *caen muertos* and the women riddled with shrapnel (*metralla*), whether they are parents or not, have, symbolically, given their child (*han dado su hijo*) to the war, *que llora y sangra en la guerra!*

# Poem XII

¡Deteneos, cañones!

¡Paraos, aviones, en mitad de vuestro inhóspito cielo!

¿No oís todos, máquinas y hombres, el llanto inmenso de todos los niños huérfanos del mundo?

## Commentary

The sky is inhospitable (*inhóspito*) because it is full of warplanes. Conde's autograph manuscript has a third injunction inserted after this: *¡Callaos,! ametralladoras*. It is the speaker's (futile) exhortation that the weapons of war: cannon, bombers (machine-guns) would listen to the *llanto inmenso* of all the orphaned children in the world. In the manuscript original, these are *los niños huérfanos de España*. This change moves the frame of reference so that it covers all the children killed in the succeeding world war as well.

# Poem XIII

¡El Agua! El Agua lo va gritando a través de los campos: «¿Quién ha visto al niño muerto, con sus ojos azules marinos llenos de gaviotas, y sus hombros hechos amapolas, y su vientre entreabierto como un fruto?»

Y lo gritan los chopos, erguidos sobre sus troncos relucientes. Lo gritan los pájaros, asustados de cuervos y de águilas.

Porque el niño que mató la guerra ha dado su voz verde a los que lo lloran a gritos.

## Commentary

**Paragraph 1:** The dead child here may be representative of all the children killed in bombing raids, and may particularly represent children in Valencia, killed on or near the docks. The water must shout the news though the fields. The dead boy has navy blue eyes (*azul marino*), the colour of the sea, and they are full of seagulls (*gaviotas*) birds which indicate proximity to the sea. His shoulders have become like poppies (*hechos amapolas*); probably they are covered in blood and his abdomen is wide open like a fruit (*entreabierto como un fruto*), this being no doubt the site of his death wound.

**Paragraph 2:** The water is joined by the black poplar trees (*chopos*) with their shiny trunks (*troncos relucientes*) in asking the question, and by the birds, the ordinary everyday birds (*los pájaros*) who are *asustados de cuervos y de águilas*, frightened by this war which is the stuff of much more fearsome birds than they, ravens (*cuervos*) and eagles (*águilas*). The raven is linked to death and disaster, the eagle to nobility and strength. The eagle was used by Fascist Italy and the Falange in Spain and much cited in poetry on both sides of the Civil War divide as example of bravery and nobility; the two-headed eagle was also, of course, the symbol of the German Third Reich.

**Paragraph 3:** The dead child has now added his *voz verde*, his immature, unripe voice to *el Agua, los chopos, los pájaros*, these three elements of disturbed nature who lament his death. In *Mientras los hombres mueren*, the speaker describes how the bodies of the dead men become one with the earth; the child here becomes one with water, trees, birds, the air.

# Poem XIV

¿Visteis a las palomas detenerse y quedar estáticas entre sus alas, a mitad de vuelo?

¿Y escuchasteis cómo los ríos se alzaron sobre sus rodillas, soplando raíces de árboles negros?

¿No sentisteis el dolor del trigo, como olor de senos calientes, en medio de la tarde doblada?

¡Era que morían los niños entre las bombas de los aviones, bajo los obuses de los cañones del odio!

## Commentary

**Paragraph 1:** The symbolism of the dove (*paloma*) is very powerful in Catholic iconography. The image of the dove, suspended in flight, is very common in representations of the Blessed Trinity, the Baptism of Christ, the Annunciation and Coronation of the Virgin and, most importantly, the Descent of the Holy Spirit at Pentecost. More generally, the dove represents peace. The speaker's question here may even refer to a simple observation of the behaviour of doves in nature, when they stop, in a kind of ecstasy (*quedar estáticas entre sus alas*) in mid-flight (*a mitad de vuelo*). There is also an implied comparison here with those other flying entities which appear to hang in the sky: bomber aircraft.

**Paragraph 2:** The second question depicts rivers, like penitents, raising themselves up on their knees (*alzarse sobre sus rodillas*), so that they lap (*soplar*, to blow) against the dark roots (*raíces de árboles negros*). It is entirely possible, given the Christian resonance of *palomas* in the previous question, to construe these *raíces de árboles negros* as referring to the True Cross, the cross on which Christ was crucified and fragments of which pilgrims and penitents would approach on their knees in churches and sanctuaries. The use of *negro* to describe these trees/roots has also a connotation of death, the destruction caused by war.

**Paragraph 3:** The third question associates wheat (*trigo*) with the smell of breasts (*olor de senos calientes*), in the sense surely of breast milk. The Roman goddes Ceres (from which name the word cereal, in Spanish and English, is derived) was the goddess of agriculture and motherly love. In Roman times, it was customary for special, female-only rites in her honour to be celebrated. Indeed, in Christianity, it is very clear that the Blessed Virgin, as mother of humankind, derives some of her qualities from Ceres. Here, however, the wheat, and by extension, the mother-goddess is in pain (*el dolor del trigo*) and the afternoon is not beautiful, it is *doblada*, bent over as in pain.

**Paragraph 4:** The three questions posed in the previous paragraphs evoke three of the five senses: *¿Visteis?¿escuchasteis?¿No sentisteis?* and the answer is that these disruptions of nature: the doves stationary in mid-flight, the waters rising to lap against black trees, the pain of the wheatfields, are responses to the annihilation of children. She is very specific here in her description of the weapons of destruction: these are the bombs from the planes (*las bombas de los aviones*); these are the shells (*obuses*) from the artillery (*cañones*) of hatred (*del odio*).

# Poem XV

¿Vamos a enseñar a estos niños que conocen el espantoso crujido de las casas, que saben el ruido de las explosiones agrias, sobre los cuerpos calientes y frescos, Historia? ¡Dejadlos olvidar este drama; dejadlos aprender el tierno discurso de los animales en la Naturaleza; dejadlos que toquen las flores y aprendan en ellas el tesoro de gozo que es el tacto!

Ninguno que sea consciente querrá enseñar ahora Historia a la infancia. ¡Ese retorcimiento de huesos humanos, un rechinar de dientes, un humear de sangres! Y ellos lo han visto con sus ojitos de pececillos asustados...

No. Que olviden la Historia. Que jueguen, que sueñen. Nadie les nombre pueblos, ni hombres. Todos les señalen mares, nubes, plantas... Y bestias.

## Commentary

**Paragraph 1:** Here, the speaker asks what possible use it could be to teach history to these children who have lived through the consequences of bombing raids: the horrific creaking (*espantoso crujido*) of houses as they collapse, the bitter smell (*agrias*, sour) of explosives. She uses the verbs *conocer* and *saber* to indicate that these children have, in a sense, already learned the lesson of contemporary history and are indeed suffering from sensory overload, one related exclusively to violent destruction. As an antidote to this, she recommends a kind of experiential learning, based on an exposure to and appreciation of a nature untouched by the horror of war. They should watch animals interacting with nature, absorb their tender language (*el tierno discurso*); they should touch flowers and find out what a great treasure house of pleasure (*tesoro de gozo*) touch (*el tacto*) can be.

**Paragraph 2:** In this paragraph she offers a a definition of what history must mean to the children of the war: a twisting (*retorcimiento*) of human bones, a grinding or gnashing (*rechinar*) of teeth, a steaming (*humear*) of blood (*sangres*, the blood of many). Watching this, these children's little eyes (*ojitos*) have seemed like the eyes of startled little fish (*pececillos asustados*), in their innocence and incomprehension.

**Paragraph 3:** Her recommendation is that these children should now forget history, they should play and dream. No-one should mention either places or people to them, they should only be shown the elements of nature: seas, clouds, plants and animals. This final sentence appears in Conde's autograph manuscript with a caesura after *plantas*, and a new sentence *Y bestias*: 'mares, nubes, plantas... Y bestias'. In Miró's *Obra poética* (1967) the caesura is omitted and the capital Y included in what looks like a printing error, *mares, nubes, plantas Y bestias*. In Miró's *Poesía completa* (2007) the line is printed without the caesura or the capital Y, *mares, nubes, plantas y bestias*. This latter is a very attractive solution, in that it places the *bestias* at one with all the other elements of nature which she recommends for the happiness of children, and it reinforces the positive reference to *el tierno discurso de los animales* in the first paragraph. Indeed, before this *bestias* are mentioned twice. In Poem XXX (*Mientras*) she speaks of the *humildes bestias* to be sacrificed to satisfy the people's hunger, and in Poem II ('Niños') she tells the children to seek out *la* [*voz*] *de las bestias sanas y vitales*. Both of these represent the *bestias* in a positive light. However, *bestias* is a word capable of a positive and a negative meaning, and it adds to the complexity of the poem that the very last sentence should be separated off by the caesura, so that *Y bestias* allows a more equivocal ending. It may equally serve to draw a distinction between *bestias* as sentient beings and the inanimate *mares* and *nubes*, and the non-sentient *plantas*.

# Poem XVI

¡Se han quedado tan pequeños los niños sobre la tierra en cortezas de hierro estallado!... Apenas si son arruguitas de los indudables musgos, insectillos seguros de los sembrados... ¿Niños en la superficie? ¡Si no se ven desde arriba, desde los aeroplanos! ¡No se ven los niños, jamás, desde el cielo!

Y están. A miríadas. Como si el cielo, cegado de su claror de estrellas, hubiera volcado en la tierra sus constelaciones. Están aquí los niños... Muchísimos, muertos ya, entre los otros que cantan y danzan y ruedan su pavor en las charcas oscuras de los ojazos... Están. ¿Vendrán más?... ¡No, por piedad, mujeres! No tragáis más niños mientras se sigan fulminando centellas contra sus cuerpos de espiga tierna, sus amapolales corazoncillos dulces!

## Commentary

**Paragraph 1:** The speaker attempts an aerial view of the city, and tries to imagine how children must appear to a bomber crew. This perspective echoes the question posed in Poem I ('Niños'), *ningún aviador enemigo tiene niñitos* [...]*?* She concludes that the children cannot be seen (*jamás, desde el cielo!*), though they are blown to smithereens amid exploded metal shell casings (*cortezas de hierro estallado*). She says they must appear like the tiny little wrinkles (*arruguitas*) in moss (*musgos*) or the minuscule insects (*insectillos*) who swarm over sown fields (*sembrados*). She uses the adjectives *indudables* and *seguros* to describe the moss and the insects respectively, apportioning them a certainty and security the children will never have.

**Paragraph 2:** Yet, she points out that they are there, in their myriads (*miríadas*). In Classical Greek/Roman history, a myriad was a unit of ten thousand; in modern times, it implies countless numbers, like the insects and the moss wrinkles. It is as if the sky, blinded with the brightness (*claror*) of its own stars had dumped (*volcar en*) all its constellations (*constelaciones*), its myriad stars, onto the surface of the earth. All the children, those already dead and those who sing and dance in play and at the same time wheel about (*ruedan*) their own terror (*pavor*), as if it were a toy, *en las charcas oscuras de los ojazos. Las charcas* are pools, and here these pools are probably the big or widened eyes of the children (*ojazos*, augmentative of *ojos*), a contrast with the diminitive used for *ojitos de pececillos asustados* of Poem XV ('Niños'). The sense here may be that the children's eyes, widened in terror, reflect the (water-filled) craters left by the bombs, even as they play near or in them, even as they do so in a state of fear (*pavor*). She finishes by exhorting women, once again, not to bring more children into this world, not while flashes of lightning (*centellas*) are still being hurled (*fulminar*, to fulminate, to strike) at childrens' bodies which are like tender ears of corn (*espiga tierna*), and their poppy-like (*amapolales*) sweet little hearts (*corazoncillos*). The reference to espigas echoes *el dolor del trigo, como olor de senos calientes* of Poem XIV ('Niños') and *amapolales*, the description of the dead child's *hombros hechos amapolas* of Poem XIII ('Niños').

# Poem XVII

Calles, ¡juntaos! Torres, ¡doblaos sobre las calles! Mar, montañas, ¡venid
sobre la ciudad donde juegan los niños! Hay aviones en el cielo, hay muerte
en el cielo... ¡Piedras y ramas, olas y bosques, venid a guardar bajo vosotros
el río de júbilo que va dentro de las venas de los niños!

## Commentary

The speaker addresses the city, ordering it to close in upon itself in order to
protect the children. She tells the streets to join together as one (*juntaos*);
she tells the towers, which might well be the *torres alígeras* (the *Torres de
Serranos* and the *Torres de Quart* in Valencia) of 'La guerra en el puerto'
(*Mientras*), to bend over the streets (*doblaos*), providing a roof. She orders
the sea and the mountains to come in over the city to protect it because
there are bombers in the sky (*hay muerte en el cielo*). She even asks the
stones and the frogs (*ranas*), the waves and the woods to come to the aid
of the *río de júbilos*, the river of joyful things (*júbilo*, jubilation) which
courses in the veins of the children. *Júbilos* is the main title of Conde's
second collection (1934), the subtitle of which, *Poemas de niños, rosas,
animales, máquinas y vientos*, offers a clear indication of the kind of child-
like innocence explored and celebrated in her first two collections of prose
poetry, an innocence profoundly lamented in these poems.

# Poem XVIII

Tengo miedo. Tengo miedo de esos motores secos, acribillantes, que perforan, que taladran hasta el génesis el oro negro, empavonado de la noche.

Tengo miedo porque oigo el gritar de los niños volcándose en escaleras y sótanos; el alentar de las madres; y me duelen los cabellos y los pulsos oyendo a la muerte caer como si fuera lluvia que buscara árboles tiernos para crecerlos de golpe.

## Commentary

This poem appears to describe, in rather direct terms, Conde's own experience of being under bombardment. In that, it is similar to Poem XXV (*Mientras*). The *motores secos* are the engines of the bomber aircraft. The sound they make is dry (*secos*) and their other important quality is that of peppering or riddling (*acribillante*) the population of the city with their bombs and bullets. These particular raids take place at night and Conde describes how it seems as if they drill (*taladrar*) into the night until they pierce (*perforar*) as far as its origin (*génesis*) the black gold of the night. This black gold is also *empavonado*, which comes from *pavonar*, meaning to blue (as in steel, a process by which an oxide is applied to the metal to protect it from rust, the steel emerging blue-black in colour after this process). The fact that oil is often described as *oro negro* and must be drilled for, that it is oil (or its derivatives) which fuels the bombers, together with the fact that the bombers and their payloads are made of metal (*metralla*, shrapnel) and her practice of describing the bomb casings as made of *hierro* (for example the *cortezas de hierro estallado* of Poem XVI ('Niños')) demonstrate that the *oro negro, empavonado* of the night may be a bivalent image: representing both the beauty of the night and the destructive force of the death machines in the night sky. Beneath the bombardment, the children are hurled about (*volcarse*) or indeed hurl themselves about (in panic) in staircases and cellars or basements (*sótanos*), places within a

157

building where people might shelter from the bombing. This pains her in her hair (*me duelen los cabellos*) and her heartbeat (*los pulsos*). The speaker refers to her hair repeatedly in *Mientras los hombres mueren*, in that it constitutes a significant and expressive part of her being. Her hair in Poem XII (*Mientras*) is a sign of good health which should not be taken at face value as a negation of the intensity of her suffering (*Aunque mi frente sea de sol maduro y mis cabellos suban en raíces al cielo*); in Poem XVI (*Mientras*), she speaks of *el Viento, adueñándose de mis cabellos para extenderlos en rubio pañuelo de olor* as the elements make her aware of her role as prophet of her people; in the same role of prophet, she calls attention to the light (*mi luz*) escaping from her hair in Poem XXII (*Mientras*). Here, in this poem, she feels pain in her hair as she hears the bombs falling from the sky, as if they were rain seeking out young trees (*árboles tiernos*), in order to bring about a sudden growth spurt (*crecerlos de golpe*), a normal expectation in the climate of the Levante. Even so, this deadly rain will have the opposite effect on the children *volcándose en escaleras y sótanos*.

# Poem XIX

*wow*

*(lo que hizo tu padre)*

Quiero tu hijo, aviador enemigo; quiero tu hijo para enseñarle el cuerpo destrozado del mío, para que te oiga volar, con tus bombas y tus balas, sobre nuestras cabezas.

Dame tu hijo, hombre que guardas en impunidad los tuyos. Dámelo, rubio y luminoso como era el mío; quiero ver que sus labios suspiran junto a mi hijo, que en sus ojos está el llanto de terror de ti. Porque soy madre del que tú has deshecho y quiero que tú me des el tuyo intacto.

No te lo heriré. No le diré mal. Mi voz será pura y ardida para llamarlo. ¡Sólo quiero que te oiga, que sepa de tu vuelo junto a la muerte de mi hijo!

Dame tu hijo, aviador enemigo. Yo te lo guardaré cantándole junto a la tumba del mío, muerto por ti.   *en comparación al enemigo*

## Commentary

Conde's autograph manuscript concludes with this poem.

**Paragraph 1:** She returns one final time to the *aviador enemigo* with whom she first engages in Poem I ('Niños') (*ningún aviador enemigo tiene niñitos*) and whose aerial perspective she alludes to in Poem XVI ('Niños') (*no se ven desde arriba, desde los aeroplanos*). The speaker establishes a relationship between the unharmed children of the enemy bomber crew and those dead children on the ground. She would like a child of an enemy bomber pilot to understand what his father does, from the viewpoint of his victims: *para que te oiga volar, con tus bombas y tus balas.*

**Paragraph 2:** The enemy bomber pilot keeps his own children safe (*en impunidad*) while he bombs those of others. The speaker compares his living child and her dead one, both beautiful in an idealised way, *rubio y luminoso*. She would like his child to experience the same terror hers went through. This would be a terror of his own father, *que en sus ojos está*

159

*el llanto de terror de ti*. The use of the indicative rather that the subjunctive for *que en sus ojos está el llanto* underlines how clear and absolute she wishes the enemy airman's child's awareness of what her child has gone through to be. The enemy pilot has blown her child to bits (*el que tú has deshecho*) so she wants his in exchange.

**Paragraph 3:** She will not hurt him or speak roughly or say bad things to him (*decirle mal*). Her voice will be pure and valiant (*ardida*) or speak of brave or valiant matters to him. Her only wish is that he should know what his father has done: *que te oiga, que sepa de tu vuelo* and that he understands the relationship between his father's actions and the death of her child.

**Paragraph 4:** Unlike the *aviador enemigo*, she will care for her enemy's son, she will sing to him, even as she shows him the grave of the child his father has killed (*muerto por ti*). She clamours for justice and reconciliation, a reconciliation which demands that the next generation from among the enemy should recognise the wrong they have done. She does not seek revenge.

# Poem XX

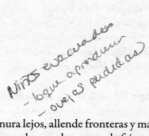

¡Cuantísimos niños balan su ternura lejos, allende fronteras y mares, de nuestra tierra! Por librarlos de la guerra les condenamos a la fría expatriación. Para evitarles la muerte de hierro, les cortamos de nuestra carne.

Aprenderán cosas ajenas en lenguas ajenas. Estrenarán su voluntad de querer en patrias distantes, otras para siempre. Inaugurarán sus brazos, sus pensamientos conscientes en países donde somos extranjeros.

Duelen esos niños que la guerra nos fuerza a salvar de su ímpetu brutal: por lejanos, porque acabarán olvidándonos, porque se les quedará la patria en la memoria, honda como un valle seco, azotado, al que temerán volver, aunque les aguarden los cadáveres de sus padres, los ojos abiertos bajo el cielo. Por salvaros, ¡ay niñitos!, nos hemos reducido hasta carecer de porvenir entre nuestros brazos.

## Commentary

This does not appear in Conde's autograph manuscript. There is a manuscript version of this poem on a loose sheet of paper. Minor but significant alterations were made to the final paragraph before its inclusion in the published version. See Appendix 3.

**Paragraph 1:** This poem is the first of two to deal with the children who were evacuated to other countries during the war. (See Introduction.) These children are like lost sheep, in that they bleat (*balar*) their tenderness (*su ternura*) a long way from home (*allende fronteras y mares*, beyond seas and across borders). The sacrifice for the adults in parting themselves from their children and sending them into cold exile (*la fría expatriación*) was like cutting off a piece of their own flesh (*les cortamos de nuestra carne*).

**Paragraph 2:** This paragraph speculates as to what these exiled children will have learned abroad, *cosas ajenas en lenguas ajenas* (alien things in alien languages). They will try out for the first time (*estrenar*) their ability to love in lands which will always be other (*otras para siempre*); they will begin to use (*inaugurar*) their arms (for work or affection) and their thoughts (*sus pensamientos conscientes*) in lands where their parents are foreigners (*donde somos extranjeros*).

**Paragraph 3:** In this final paragraph, the speaker deals with the fears which must have haunted every parent who sent a child away to protect him or her from the brutality (*ímpetu brutal*) of war: of their being far away (*por lejanos*), of their forgetting their parents (*acabarán olvidándonos*), of the memory of their homeland being buried deep in their memories like a dry and weatherbeaten (*azotado*) valley, so much so that they will be afraid to return. *Aunque les aguarden los cadáveres de sus padres* implies that it would be a sacred duty, nevertheless, to return to pay their respects to their dead parents, if they could. Her conclusion is that the people have, in acting to save their children's lives, deprived themselves of a future. There will now be no future to hold in their arms, *hasta carecer de porvenir entre nuestros brazos*.

# Poem XXI

¡Traed a los niños! *tuera*

En los mismos aviones de la guerra, en los barcos que llevaron y trajeron toneladas de llanto. Traedlos desde las lluvias lejanas, desde los suelos ásperos, a su sol y a sus frutos, a sus madres y a sus padres vivos y a sus muertos.

Traednos los niños que perdieron en sus bocas la alegría de nuestro idioma. A todos los que sacamos entre bombas, sirenas, cañonazos, espantados de que en su patria se les arrojara a la muerte o al extranjero. ¡Madres jóvenes de España, pedid a vuestros hijos! No les habléis de la guerra. Que olviden (como cuando nada sabían en vuestros vientres) cuánto lloramos por ellos.

¡Traednos a los niños, hombres vencedores! Necesitamos su antorcha sobre nuestras frentes.

## Commentary

This does not appear in Conde's autograph manuscript. In this second poem, now that the war is over, the speaker asks for the return of the exiled children. They should be returned in those same machines which caused their exile in the first place: the *aviones de la guerra*, the *barcos* which brought and took away *toneladas de llanto* (tonnes of suffering), presumably the ships of the Nationalist navy which shelled the city, the other ships which took the children away into exile. The children must return to their own land, characterised by sun and fruit, and to their parents, living or dead, from their places of exile, which may have had relatively harsh climates (*suelos ásperos*) or more temperate ones (*las lluvias lejanas*). She anticipates that these children may have forgotten how to speak Spanish (*que perdieron en sus bocas la alegría de nuestro idioma*), she recognises that they were horrified (*espantados*) by a land which cast (*arrojar*) them in the path of death or into exile. Finally, now that there is peace, she can exhort the mothers of Spain to ask for their children back, but, as she instructs in

Poem XV ('Niños'), they should hear nothing of the war and they should be allowed to forget, or never to know, how much the adults suffered from their absence (*cuánto lloramos por ellos*). Her last plea is to the victors, *hombres vencedores,* that they should bring the children back. The people need the light of these children, a torch (*antorcha,* torch, a more domesticated kind, not always using a naked flame, as distinct from *tea* which she has used up to now) on their faces (*nuestras frentes*). As history proved, this was a somewhat forlorn hope. (See Armengou and Belis, *Los niños perdidos del franquismo* (Barcelona: Plaza y Janés, 2002).)

# Appendices

## Appendix 1: Final two paragraphs of No. XXVI (*Mientras*) from the manuscript original

Yo camino por entre las piedras de las viejas casas españolas que deshacen las bombas, que derriban los obuses... Si al fin yo sobresalí de mi mapa no fue por la historia del Arte antiguo, no fue por la felicidad, ni por el amor; es por la guerra.

Acabamos de encontrarnos en un abrazo estrecho, eterno, vosotros y yo. Llevádme mis ojos manchados de sangre, del esplendor dorado de vuestras ruinas que yo no conozco.

## Commentary

In the first paragraph the speaker makes a rare reference to the specific Spanish context of the war, *las casas españolas*, and implies a comparison between these houses destroyed by bombs and shells (*obuses*) and Herculaneum and Pompeii, destroyed by the forces of nature. She explains that she finally emerged from her map of learning about the ancient world based on books, maps and globes because of the war; neither love nor happiness would have forced her to such a renunciation of learning for its own sake. In the second paragraph, there is a meeting between the speaker and the people of these ancient ruins; they now have destruction in common, and she asks them to take her away now, her eyes stained with blood from (contemplation of) the *esplendor dorado de vuestras ruinas*, which of course she has never actually seen.

**Appendix 2: Manuscript version of 'Ha terminado la guerra'**
(*Mientras*)

Han aullado los barcos, y en los sombríos muelles las torrenciales agonías de millares de hombres que querían huir, vencidos. Dichosos desdichados los que alcanzaron nave que les expatriara! Cuántos, aquí, llorando la derrota caminaban con sed y con hambre, sin dinero, sin mano amiga que les diera consuelo para su aflición!

Como un alud inmensísimo, terminó la guerra; se desplomó la paz. Frenesí de banderas otras, de gritos, de reivindicaciones. Estallido de la victoria colosal de hermanos fuertes sobre hermanos débiles.

Los harrapientos, los miserables, los que soñaban una redención sobre la que especulaban extraños cuyos únicos signos eran el oro, el mercurio, el aceite, la almendra, la naranja...; todos los embriagados con ideales traicionados por delincuentes, todos los crédulos de revoluciones que esperaban puras, se han hundido en una eternidad de sangre.


**Commentary**

The published poem is much pithier than this version. Apart from some minor changes to vocabulary, however, it is made up of the first four sentences of this version.

**Paragraph 1:** In the second sentence, the *dichosos desdichados* (fortunate unfortunates) become *los audaces*, a more positive gloss, in the published version. Conde uses the verb *expatriar*, to expatriate or take into exile, here. In the published version, she uses the more neutral *salvar*. In the third sentence, there is no initial exclamation mark. This may be deliberate or an oversight in the original.

**Paragraph 2:** Everything after the first sentence in this paragraph is omitted from the final version. In the second sentence, *banderas otras*, refers to the Nationalist flags, now flying in Valencia, and to the demands (*reivindicaciones*) of the victors. She portrays this victory as an explosion (*estallido*) of colosal victory (*la victoria colosal*) of stronger men over their weaker brothers.

**Paragraph 3:** This final paragraph contains one of her most bitter condemnations of the greedy and selfish behaviour of human beings during the war. The idealistic have lost out, they are now in rags (*harrapientos*) and misery (*miserables*) because they dreamt of a better, more just society (*soñaban una redención*). In fact, their political idealism, or even naivety, was speculated upon, from the outset, by outsiders or strangers (*sobre la que especulaban extraños*), in other words entrepreneurs, among whom there were many Spanish nationals, who were making profits at the Republican government's expense. Instead of flags, these people had for identifying symbols (*signos*) the commodities in which they speculated. These ranged from precious metals to ordinary crops: gold, mercury, (cooking and fuel) oil, almonds, oranges. Thus, all those drunk (*embriagados*) on ideals saw themselves and their ideals betrayed (*traicionados*) by those she terms *delincuentes*. All those who believed in (*los crédulos*) a pure revolution were, instead, submerged (*hundirse*) in *una eternidad de sangre*.

## Appendix 3: Manuscript version of No. XX ('Niños'): paragraphs 3 and 4

Duelen esos niños que la guerra fuerza a salvar de su bárbaro ímpetu, por lejanos, porque acabarán olvidándonos. Porque se les quedará España en la memoria honda, como un valle seco, azotado, al que temerán volver aunque les aguarden los cadáveres de sus padres insepultos, los ojos abiertos contra el cielo insensibilizado.

Por salvaros, ay niñitos españoles, nos hemos reducido tánto que carecemos de porvenir entre nuestros brazos.

1939 Valencia.


### Commentary

In the first sentence, *bárbaro* becomes *brutal* in the published version. In the second, *España* becomes *la patria*, *insepultos* (unburied) is withdrawn from *los cadáveres*, and *los ojos abiertos contra el cielo insensibilizado* (desensitised) is changed to the simpler *los ojos bajo el cielo*. What constitutes the fourth paragraph here is incorporated into the third and final paragraph in the published version. The adjective *españoles* is omitted, rendering the nationality of the *niñitos* less specific and the construction with *carecer* is simplified, from *nos hemos reducido tánto que carecemos de porvenir*, with *tánto* providing a rhetorical urgency, to the more sober *nos hemos reducido hasta carecer de porvenir*.

In all three instances where there are differences between the manuscript and the published versions, it seems that Conde has acted to reduce the specificity of the poems, so that, in keeping with her preface, they reflect the destruction visited on all cities in the wars of the 1930s and 1940s in Europe and the rest of the world. She has also toned down the emotionalism of the poems, made the language sparser and more sombre, the outcome no doubt of living through over a decade of Francoism and the Second World War before these poems were finally prepared for publication in Italy in 1953.

# Temas de debate y discusión

*Mientras los hombres mueren*

1  ¿Qué papel quiere desempeñar la narradora/poeta frente al pueblo de su patria?

2  ¿Cómo enfoca la narradora/poeta la relación entre los cadáveres de los soldados muertos y la Naturaleza?

3  ¿Qué significado tiene la oposición luz/sombra en estos poemas?

4  ¿Cómo representa la poeta al héroe? ¿Puede serlo una mujer?

5  ¿Según la narradora/poeta, cuál es la responsabilidad de la mujer joven en tiempos de guerra? ¿Por qué?

6  ¿Qué significado tiene el mar/la mar en estos poemas?

7  ¿Cómo ve la narradora/poeta el futuro de los vencedores en la posguerra? ¿el de los fugitivos/vencidos?

## 'A los niños muertos en la guerra'

1  ¿Se nota una diferencia entre la representación del niño y de la niña en estos poemas? ¿Cómo se define esta diferencia?

2  ¿Cómo ve la narradora/poeta al aviador enemigo?

3  ¿Cómo representa la ciudad bajo el bombardeo enemigo?

4  ¿Cómo imagina el regreso de los niños exiliados? ¿y la reacción de los adultos sobrevivientes?

# Selected vocabulary

abismo, abyss
abrasar, to burn
acompasar, to be in step, keep in
    rhythm
acorrer, to rush to assist (some-
    one)
acribillante, peppering (with
    shot)
acribillar, to pepper (with shot)
acudir, to attend
adelantado, a moving forwards
adueñarse de, to take over
afilado, sharpened
agonizante, dying, in agony
agraz, unripe grape
agrio, bitter, sour
aguardar, to wait, to expect
águila, eagle
ahincosamente, diligently
ajado, worn
ajeno, removed from, alien
ala, wing
alameda, a tree-lined road, avenue
alarido, clamouring, scream
alba, dawn
alboroto, commotion
alcanzar, to reach
alentar, to encourage, hearten
alíjera, winged
aliviar, to alleviate, relieve
allende, beyond

alud, landslide, avalanche
alumbrar, to light up
alzar, to raise up
amamantar, to suckle
amapola, poppy
amapolal, poppy-like
anegar, to flood or overwhelm
angustia, anguish
anhelante, longing
antorcha, torch
anudar, to tie (together)
apaciguar, to pacify, sate
apretar, to press
arbolar, to raise up, lift up
arboleda, grove
arder, to burn
ardido, burning, ardent
arranque, fit
arrasante, devastating
arrasar, to brush, blow away
arrebato, fit
arrojarse, to throw (oneself)
arrostrar, to confront
arroyo, stream
arruga, wrinkle
ascua, ember
asfalto, asphalt
asordado, deafened
asordar, to deafen
áspero, rough, coarse
asustadizo, easily scared

**atender**, to pay attention
**atezado**, bronzed, tanned
**atronador**, thundering
**augusto**, august; noble and splendid
**aullar**, to howl
**azotado**, whipped
**azotar**, to whip, scourge
**bala**, bullet
**balar**, to bleat, baa
**barca**, small boat, rowboat
**barco**, large boat, ship
**barrer**, to sweep
**barro**, mud
**bergantín**, brigantine
**blando**, soft, smooth
**blanducho**, flabby
**bosque**, wood, coppice
**bóveda**, vault
**bramar**, to roar
**brasas**, embers
**bronco**, gruff
**bruñido**, burnished
**cabalgar**, to ride (a horse)
**cabellera**, lock (of hair)
**calar**, to seep, penetrate
**campana**, bell, bell-shaped vessel
**cañón**, big gun, field artillery, cannon
**cañonazo**, cannon fire
**cántico**, canticle
**caracola**, conch shell
**carecer**, to lack
**casco**, shell
**cascote**, shell, casing
**caudal**, flow (river); wealth
**celo**, zeal, lust
**centella**, a flash (of lightning)
**cercanía**, locality, nearness

**charca**, pool
**chatarra**, scrap (metal)
**chirriante**, screeching
**chispa**, sparks, **en chispas**, on fire
**chopo**, black poplar
**cifra**, number, cypher
**cimbrearse**, to sway
**cintura**, waist
**claror**, brightness, glow
**clavar**, to nail
**compañía**, company
**conjurar**, to summon (a spirit)
**constelación**, constellation
**contienda**, struggle, battle
**contrapunto**, counterpoint
**corcel**, steed
**corro**, pit, circle
**corteza**, cortex, bark, shell
**costado**, side, ribs
**crespón**, mourning ribbon
**crin**, mane (horse)
**cruce**, crossroads
**crujidor**, rustling
**crujir**, to crunch, rustle
**cruz**, cross
**cuajar**, to set
**cuenco**, hollow
**cuerpo a cuerpo**, hand-to-hand
**cuervo**, raven
**cuesta**, hill
**cuna**, cradle
**deflorado**, deflowered (virginity)
**delirante**, delirious
**deponer**, to lay down, put away
**derramar**, to spill
**derrota**, defeat
**derrumbar**, to tear down, demolish
**desarraigado**, uprooted

**desbandado**, disbanded, dispersed

**desbaratar**, to disrupt, ruin

**desbocado**, out of control

**descargar**, to unload

**descuajar**, to unseat, uproot, displace

**desdichado**, unfortunate (person)

**desenfreno**, lack of control, abandon

**desfrutecido**, not having borne fruit or being prevented from doing so

**desgajar(se)**, to break away, tear off

**desgarrado**, torn

**desgarrador**, tearing

**desgranar**, to crumb, shell, pod

**desguarnecida**, ungarrisoned, undefended

**deshabitado**, uninhabited

**deshielo**, thawing

**deshojar**, to tear the leaves off

**designio**, plan, design

**deslumbrado**, dazzled (by light)

**desmedido**, unmeasured, immeasurable

**desorbitado**, wide-open in shock

**desparramado**, spilt, spattered (on)

**despavorido**, terrified

**desplomarse**, to collapse

**despojado**, stripped (of)

**desprender**, to detach, set loose

**desvelado**, sleepless

**desvencijado**, rickety, dilapidated

**diana**, target

**dicha**, good fortune

**dichoso**, fortunate

**dilatar**, to dilate, expand

**dislocarse**, to dislocate, go mad

**dispar**, uneven, ill-matched

**don**, a gift

**duelo**, pain, suffering, sorrow, mental torment

**ébano**, ebony

**eludir**, to elude

**embriaguez**, intoxication

**empapado**, soaked

**empapar**, to soak

**empavonar**, to blue (steel)

**empolvado**, dust-covered

**encía**, gum (mouth)

**encogerse**, to shrink (into oneself)

**enhiesto**, upright

**enlosado**, paved

**enmarañado**, tangled up (in)

**ensueño**, dream, ideal

**enterrado**, buried

**entumecido**, numb, stiff

**erguir**, to raise up

**escucha**, lookout, scout

**escurrido**, sagging, flattened

**esfera**, sphere, planet

**esgrimir**, to wield, brandish

**espanto**, shock, horror, fright

**espantoso**, horrifying

**espasmo**, spasm

**espesor**, density, thickness

**espiga**, an ear of wheat, oats, barley (usually wheat)

**espoleta**, fuse

**estallido**, explosion

**estampido**, bang, report

**estanque**, pool

**estertor**, death rattle

**estremecer (se)**, to shudder

**estremecimiento**, shudder (usually pleasureable)
**estrenar**, to try out, show
**estrépito**, din, loud noise
**estridencial**, strident, clamouring
**estridente**, strident
**estrujado**, squeezed dry
**fangoso**, muddy
**fardo**, bale (of merchandise)
**fibras**, fibres
**fragor**, roar (heat of battle)
**frenesí**, frenzy
**frenético**, frenetic, a crazy person
**friso**, frieze
**frondoso**, leafy
**fugaz**, swift, fleeting
**fulminar**, to fulminate
**furibundo**, furious, enraged
**galopar**, gallop
**gaviota**, seagull
**gemido**, trembling, shuddering
**gozo**, pleasure
**grano**, grain
**grasiento**, greasy
**hachazo**, hatchet blow
**harrapiento**, ragged, in rags
**haz**, sheaf (of corn)
**heces**, (pl.) ordure, manure
**hectáreas**, hectares
**helicoidal**, spiral-shaped
**hélix**, propeller
**henchir**, to expand, swell
**hendidor**, causing (something) to split
**hermético**, hermetic, sealed off
**hiedra**, ivy
**hincar**, to thrust (into)
**horadar**, to drill (through)

**humear**, to (emit) steam, smoke
**hundidor**, causing (something) to sink
**hundir**, to sink
**impávido**, fearless, undaunted
**ímpetu**, impetus, force
**imprecación**, imprecation, curse
**imprescindible**, indispensable
**impunidad**, impunity
**inaugurar**, to inaugurate
**incendiar**, to set fire (to)
**incendio**, large fire, bonfire
**incorporarse**, to become
**infructuosamente**, fruitlessly
**inmensurable**, immeasurable
**insensato**, insensible, unaware
**insepulto**, unburied
**investido**, invested (with)
**jarcias**, rigging (ship)
**júbilo**, jubilation, joy
**lámina**, plate (illustration)
**latido**, heartbeat
**lecho**, bed, deathbed
**legado**, legacy
**lienzo**, canvas (painting)
**limo**, mud
**llaga**, wound
**llama**, flame
**llano**, plain
**lucero**, bright star
**lujuria**, lust
**lumbre**, light, glow
**machacar**, to crush
**marejada**, great ocean wave
**mármol**, marble
**mazorca**, corn cob
**mechón**, lock (of hair)
**meseta**, high plateau
**metralla**, shrapnel

**miembro,** member (part of the body)

**miríada,** myriad

**morado,** deep reddish purple

**muchedumbre,** crowd

**muralla,** city wall

**musgo,** moss

**navío,** large (cargo) ship

**obus,** shell or cannon

**odres,** wineskins

**oleada,** wave

**óleo,** oil

**ordeñar,** to milk

**orilla,** bank (river), edge

**pabellón,** pavilion

**pacer,** to graze

**par,** even (number); paired

**parcamente,** in a frugal way

**parir,** to give birth

**partir,** to split

**parturienta,** (in the act of) giving birth

**pavesa,** soot particle

**pavor,** fear, terror

**perennidad,** quality of being everlasting

**pergamino,** parchment

**pervivir,** to endure, survive

**petrificado,** petrified, turned to stone

**pezón,** nipple

**pineal,** pineal (gland)

**piramidales,** pyramid-shaped

**plantas,** plants or feet

**pleamar,** high tide

**plomo,** lead

**podrido,** rotten

**pólvora,** gunpowder

**pórfido,** porphyry

**postrero,** last, final

**presentir,** presentiment, premonition

**prevalecer,** to prevail

**propicio,** opportune

**prorrumpir,** to burst out

**próvido,** provident

**púa,** barb, spike, needle, quill

**puñal,** dagger

**punzador,** punchy, punching

**punzante,** biting

**pupila,** pupil (eye)

**quebrar,** to break, shatter

**quejido,** groan

**quilla,** keel

**racimo,** cluster

**raíz,** root

**rajar,** to tear, rip

**realzar,** to raise up again

**rebanadas,** thin strips

**rebaño,** flock or herd

**rebosante,** brimming over (with)

**rechinar,** to grind, gnash

**recobrar,** to recover

**regazo,** lap

**reivindicación,** demand

**relojería,** clockwork (mechanism)

**reluciente,** shiny

**rematar,** to end up

**repicador,** ringing

**reseco,** very dry

**resollado,** out of breath

**resollar,** to pant

**resquebrajante,** cracking, splitting

**restallante,** cracked, parched

**retorcer,** to twist

**retorcimiento,** twisting

**retroceso,** a pulling backwards

**reventado**, burst
**riachuelo**, small stream
**rodar**, to roll, wheel
**romance**, ballad; describes a
  Latin-based language
**ronco**, hoarse
**rudo**, tough
**salor**, brine
**seguridad**, security
**selva**, forest or jungle
**sembrado**, sown or planted field
**seno**, breast (women)
**serenidad**, serenity
**serpear**, to wind
**sien**, temple (skull)
**simiente**, seed
**sin fin**, something which has no
  end
**sino**, destiny
**sobresaltar**, to take by surprise
**soledad**, solitude, aloneness
**sombrío**, dark
**soplar**, to lap against
**sorber**, to suck
**sosiego**, peace (of mind)
**sótano**, cellar
**súbitamente**, suddenly
**sucumbir**, to succumb
**sufridor**, sufferer, suffering
**sujetar**, to hold (up or down)
**surtir**, to spring up
**suspiro**, sigh
**sustentar**, to sustain
**tácito**, understood (but not
  expressed)
**tajo**, gorge, ravine, slash
**taladrar**, to drill
**tañir**, to pluck (a stringed

instrument)
**tea**, torch (with a naked flame)
**telúrica**, telluric, of the earth
**tenebroso**, dark, shadowy
**tifón**, typhoon
**torreón**, large tower
**trajinar**, to rush about
**transido**, wracked (by)
**trastornado**, upset, disturbed
**trigo**, wheat
**trilita (trinitrolueno)**, TNT
  (trinitrotoluene, a powerful
  explosive)
**triturar**, to chew (on)
**triza**, shred
**trizar**, to smash to pieces
**ufanía**, self-satisfaction,
  smugness
**umbral**, shade, shadow
**unánime**, unanimous
**vaivén**, toing and froing, swaying,
  moving up and down
**vasija**, vessel, container
**velado**, veiled, hidden
**velero**, sailing ship
**venero**, vein, seam in the soil
**vigilia**, vigilance
**vísceras**, entrails, guts, insides
**viscoso**, viscous
**volcarse de**, to jump (out of), **en**
  (into)
**voraz**, voracious
**vulnerar**, to wound
**yacer**, to lie (in death)
**yelos**, ice (**hielo**); severe frost
**zanja**, ditch, trench
**zumbar**, to hum
**zumo**, juice